GW01417846

Pubs
that welcome
Children
Jimmy Young

David & Charles
Newton Abbot · London · North Pomfret (Vt)

CONTENTS

ISBN 0-7153-7965-8

© Text: Jimmy Young 1980
© Maps: David & Charles 1980

Typeset by Photoprint, Paignton
and Printed in Great Britain
by Butler & Tanner Limited, Frome
for David & Charles (Publishers) Limited
Brunel House Newton Abbot Devon

Published in the United States of America
by David & Charles Inc
North Pomfret Vermont 05053 USA

All rights reserved. No part of this
publication may be reproduced, stored in
a retrieval system, or transmitted, in any
form or by any means, electronic,
mechanical, photocopying, recording or
otherwise, without the prior permission
of David & Charles (Publishers) Limited

INTRODUCTION

It was during the International Year of the Child that I did the research for this brief guide. To cover the country with my prepared lists I travelled 11,100 miles in England and 1,400 in Wales. I visited over 800 pubs, some at 8.30 am when the cleaning lady was in, others in the middle of the afternoon, when normally the landlord expects peace and quiet, and I was still going at closing time most evenings! Of these 800 pubs I called at, some had no legal rooms, others did not wish the publicity as they had enough trade. Generally I did not call on town pubs, partly because of parking problems, and also because in towns there are generally enough hotels which cater for children.

I have divided the pubs into two sections. First, there are pubs with children's facilities and rooms for wet weather, all of which I have visited and selected — 590 in all. Secondly there are pubs reputed to have facilities for children, of which I have listed approximately 1,160, taken from lists supplied by many of the breweries or from various national, regional and county guides that I have amongst my collection of nearly 800 books and pamphlets.

I have located by no means all the pubs which welcome children in all weathers and seasons. Some of these I have listed under the heading 'Other Pubs to Try' and where they are reputed to have a family/ children's room I have used the term 'children's facilities'.

The idea was sown by the Marketing Manager of David & Charles when discussing the details of my first national guide *Services On and Off the Motorways*. Unsponsored and independent of any outside influence, I have visited every pub I list, be it only briefly: I have seen all the rooms which can be used by families with their children; some are luxurious, many adequate, some only pokey little places, but nevertheless adequate to satisfy the law.

In my younger days, pubs had many rooms, some of which had no bars; it was possible to take one's children (or grandchildren) out, and enjoy a Sunday pint or a holiday drink, depositing them in some back room off the passage. Gone are those days with the small intimate bars; these rooms have been joined into one or two bars for 'easier supervision', so using every inch of floor space. No thought has been given to the future drinking population, who well remember their introduction to the pub through the side entrance or the passage, the ginger pop or orangeade (nowadays Cokes) brought to them while sitting quietly enjoying the privilege of being taken out. While at school many of us have run the risk of expulsion while having half a pint of shandy in a favourite back room of a quiet pub while the masters were in the lounge bar next door. Nowadays many a youth over 16 and entitled to bottled shandy is excluded from pubs altogether. I remember with surprise the day when a regular youngster came in to the pub of which I was landlord and ordered a double brandy. When I asked if he was ill he said 'No', but explained that he was celebrating his eighteenth birthday. (For over a year he had been drinking beer and had come in occasionally with his parents.) It is often impossible to discern the teenager's exact age, and one has to rely on his word that he is over eighteen and entitled to the full privileges of a pub.

Very few breweries make any effort to aid their landlords to help parents with children in their tied houses. Certain areas of the country are very sparsely served in this respect and few of the new houses have been designed with any idea of a family room. This, surely, is a very short-sighted policy, especially with the recommendations in the Errol Report, which sooner or later will be implemented in a modified way. Some of the national and regional brewers are, however, realising the need for children's facilities at their pubs. They are converting existing pubs, putting back a small room; Allied Breweries are in the process of introducing Wayfarer Inns which cater especially for parents with families, and have gone in for elaborate play areas outdoors as well as very adequate rooms indoors. Bass are not so elaborate but are encouraging their tenants and managers, where suitable houses exist, to make provision for families. The other national breweries leave it to their landlords to use their own initiative.

Of the regional breweries, Devenish in Cornwall are making provision for rooms in many houses, carrying out major improvements so that these can be used as family rooms if the landlord so desires. Hall and Woodhouse, Eldridge Pope, Charles Wells and Greenall Whitley help any landlord in developing family facilities in his pub if he presses them hard enough. So some breweries are beginning to take an interest in the future generation of customers.

Although I have seen or communicated with all the breweries in the country, these seem to be the only ones taking an active interest at the moment: others have intimated they could be looking at the problem in the future. However, the great majority seem to think that the pub is for drinking only, and such it should remain. This is also the view of some landlords. Surely, however, the youngsters remember the pub where, as children, they drank their Coke, romped on the lawns, watched the telly in the family room while their parents had a relaxing break and a welcome drink.

Brewers and landlords themselves could obviate a lot of frustration to the customer by converting sheds and barns into homely little rooms, sparsely furnished, which would meet the requirements of the law. Such rooms could then be utilised for family games rooms, as many pubs are now doing, often installing a pool table.

There is a strong feeling amongst some publicans about children being in pubs at all. This is, nowadays, both narrow-minded and impracticable. Had hooligans had more parental care, being allowed and encouraged to go out and about with their families, some of the present-day troubles would no doubt have been curbed. Parents, nowadays, have much more care and affection for their children, taking them around on holidays and at weekends. On fine days, it is fairly easy when on holiday to entertain and amuse the children, but in wet weather and in the winter where can one go? The pub — but which one? Some landlords will take pity on you and so break the law (putting his licence in jeopardy) allowing you to sit in a corner with the children: the next time the parent takes it for granted that the landlord will always allow a child in and takes his family to that pub without asking if it is all right: others who have children see this, and so bring their own. The landlord then puts his foot down, and so offends the parents and consequently loses good customers.

The landlord has the right, and sole discretion, to refuse entry to his establishment without giving reason for his refusal, and may ask anyone on his premises to leave at any time. By law he is forbidden to serve anyone who seems drunk on his premises. It is an offence for an adult to be in charge of a child whilst drunk.

I give extracts from the law so that the public may be aware of it, and so that the many landlords who are under the apprehension that children are not allowed on licensed premises at all can sort out which rooms would be appropriate if they so wished: some of the brewers and their representatives have little or no knowledge of this aspect of its application.

Laws

The 1964 Act, Section 168, states 'the holder of a justices' licence shall not allow a person under fourteen to be *in the bar of licensed premises* during the permitted hours'.

'Where it was shown that a person under fourteen was *in the bar* of any licensed premises during the permitted hours, the holder of the justices' licence shall be guilty . . . unless he proves . . . that he used due diligence to prevent the person under fourteen from being admitted to the bar', and may be fined up to £25.

'No offence shall be committed if the person under fourteen . . . is in the bar *solely for the purpose* of passing to and from some part of the premises which is not a bar and to or from which there is no other convenient means of access or egress.'

This means that children under fourteen may be in any part of licensed premises other than the bar, without an offence being committed.

The definition of 'bar' requires that the sale and consumption of intoxicating liquor is the primary use of that room. A games room across the passage from the bar (even if full of drinkers, provided they have to fetch and pay for their drinks in another room) would suffice. If drinks are brought to that room and money collected at the time of serving by the landlord or his agents the room could then be said to be a bar.

A room which has been habitually used as a bar (usually with a counter) does not cease to be a bar if closed for a period for a disco or other function if held *during permitted hours,* even if no intoxicating liquor is sold.

A children's room as such has no substance in law, but is easily set aside for the purpose and is a solution to the problem of inclement weather, as are rooms set aside for the primary purpose of serving food.

Children under eighteen may not buy or consume alcoholic liquor *on licensed premises* at any time. Children over sixteen may consume beer, porter, cider or perry at a meal in a part of the premises which is not a bar, usually set aside for the service of meals.

Under the existing licensing laws there is no restriction on street drinking outside a pub (but other civil charges such as obstruction, or causing a nuisance, may be incurred).

There is no existing law (as in other countries) against drinking in a vehicle, but,

DO NOT DRINK AND DRIVE

As far as I can ascertain no successful prosecution has been instigated against landlords for allowing children on licensed premises during permitted hours in the last fifteen years. Maybe this is because it is very hard to prove such cases, or because the police do not consider that such cases justify more than a caution to the landlord.

The above laws are all subject to the landlord's consent; he is the sole adjudicator as to who shall enter his pub, whatever age, creed or colour. He is the king of his castle (an Englishman's home is his castle, and the pub is the landlord's home as well as his livelihood). His representatives (bar staff, etc) are included in the term 'landlord'.

Hotels

All licensed hotels should have foyers, lobbies, or a lounge in which residents or the general public may sit with their children (with the proprietor's discretion to refuse admission). Any child is allowed in the restaurant, dining room or a hotel to eat. The Trades Description Act has defined hotels, but pubs still refer to themselves as hotels though they offer no accommodation and little food, and keep open only during the licensing hours. Some brewers have dropped the word 'hotel' from their pubs, many of which did provide accommodation until very stringent fire precautions were introduced), but many have not. (The same applies to an 'inn' which term may be taken to indicate that food and accommodation are available.)

Restaurants

Licensed restaurants are similar to hotels. Any child is allowed in to eat and may sit in the bar area waiting for a meal to be prepared whether accompanied or not. This also applies to restaurants in pubs, many of which probably have a special hours certificate allowing longer opening hours. Again, the hotelier or restauranteur has full authority to refuse admission without giving any reason.

I have not included in my featured pubs hotels, many of which welcome children and have lovely gardens with swings, swimming pools and special play-rooms with games and TV. No mention is made of restaurants which serve children's portions, have high-chairs available for babies, and prepare baby food, though there are many which do have these facilities. This is solely a pub guide selecting some of the finest pubs in each county (and a few not-so-nice, but still offering a service), where children are welcome. It is by no means a complete survey, and as landlords retire and are replaced some of the pubs may no longer be so willing to have children. At the time of the survey the particulars were correct. Neither my publishers nor I can be held responsible for any inaccuracies that may be found, though every care has been taken to depict the pubs as found by me. If you are travelling any distance it is advisable to phone the landlord and check that he still has a children's/family room available.

My thanks are due to many of the national and regional brewers on whom I have called, who have told me which of their pubs would be worth a visit, or who have sent me lists of pubs with children's amenities; to the authors and editors of numerous national, regional and local guides from which I have been able to locate pubs with children's facilities, so enabling me to have a nucleus of pubs on which to call: to the landlords who have answered my questions, often out of opening hours, and shown me their facilities for children: to their customers who have told me of other houses in the area (often, alas, leading me some 10 or 20 miles on a wild-goose chase, as the pub had no legal room or had given up the children's room); to Peggy Burgess who checked on details I forgot to note, and typed the manuscript for my publishers; to Pam Darlaston who has done so much behind the scenes editing my script; and to you, the reader, who I hope will find the pubs as helpful as I did.

Specially recommended pubs with excellent facilities for children are marked **. Pubs recommended for the whole family are marked *.

I would be glad to have any comments on pubs throughout the country which have children's amenities, so that they may be noted in any reprint.

Jimmy Young
Red Cross House
Crediton
Devon

10

NORTHUMBERLAND

TYNE & WEAR

DURHAM

CLEVELAND

CUMBRIA

9

8

NORTH YORKSHIRE

LANCASHIRE

W YORKS

HUMBERSIDE

MERSEYSIDE

GREATER MANCHESTER

S YORKS

7

CHESHIRE

DERBY

NOTTINGHAM

LINCOLN

CLWYD

6

GWYNEDD

STAFFORD

SALOP

5

LEICESTER

NORFOLK

MIDLANDS

WARWICK

NORTHAMPTON

CAMBRIDGE

SUFFOLK

4

POWYS

HEREFORD & WORCESTER

BEDS

DYFED

GLOUCESTER

OXFORD

BUCKS

HERTS

ESSEX

W GLAM

MID. GLAM

GWENT

GREATER LONDON

3

S GLAM

AVON

WILTS

BERKS

SURREY

KENT

SOMERSET

HANTS

DEVON

DORSET

W SUSSEX

E SUSSEX

2

CORNWALL

7

MAP 1   8

MAP 1

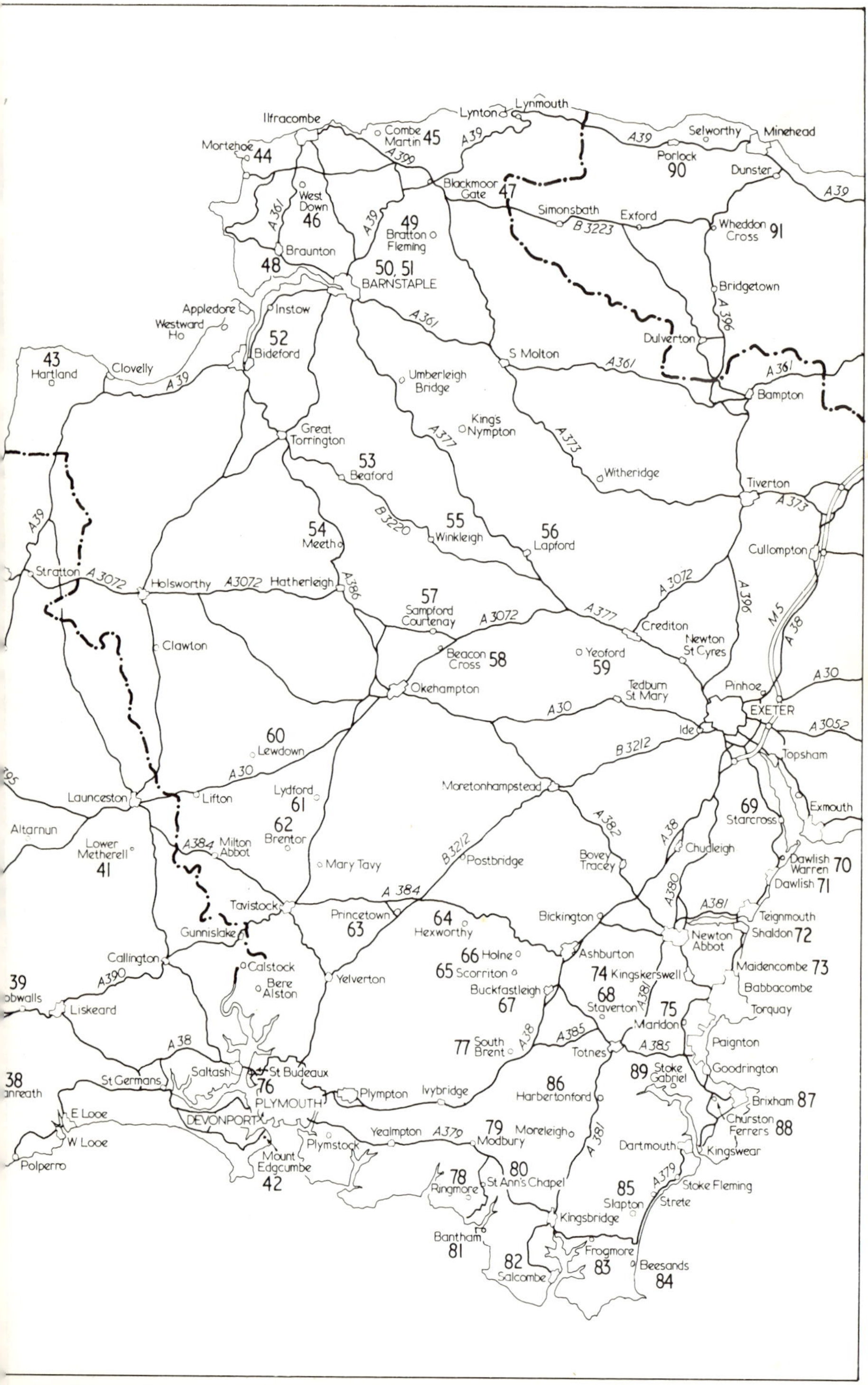
Ilfracombe
Mortehoe 44
Combe Martin 45
Lynton
Lynmouth
Selworthy
Minehead
Porlock 90
Dunster
Blackmoor Gate 47
West Down 46
Braunton
48
Bratton Fleming 49
50, 51 BARNSTAPLE
Simonsbath
Exford
Wheddon Cross 91
Bridgetown
Appledore
Instow
Westward Ho
52 Bideford
43 Hartland
Clovelly
Dulverton
S Molton
Umberleigh Bridge
Bampton
Great Torrington
King's Nympton
53 Beaford
Witheridge
Tiverton
54 Meeth
55 Winkleigh
56 Lapford
Cullompton
Stratton
Holsworthy
Hatherleigh
57 Sampford Courtenay
Crediton
Newton St Cyres
Clawton
Beacon Cross 58
Yeoford 59
Okehampton
Tedburn St Mary
Pinhoe
EXETER
Ide
Topsham
60 Lewdown
Launceston
Lifton
Lydford 61
62 Brentor
Moretonhampstead
69 Starcross
Exmouth
Altarnun
Lower Metherell 41
Milton Abbot
Mary Tavy
Postbridge
Bovey Tracey
Chudleigh
Dawlish Warren 70
Dawlish 71
Tavistock
Princetown 63
64 Hexworthy
Bickington
Teignmouth
Gunnislake
Newton Abbot
Shaldon 72
Callington
Calstock
66 Holne
Ashburton
Maidencombe 73
39
Bere Alston
Yelverton
65 Scorriton
74 Kingskerswell
Babbacombe
Liskeard
Buckfastleigh 67
68 Staverton
Torquay
75 Marldon
77 South Brent
Totnes
Paignton
38
Saltash
St Budeaux
76
PLYMOUTH
St Germans
89 Stoke Gabriel
Goodrington
Plympton
Ivybridge
86 Harbertonford
Brixham 87
E Looe
DEVONPORT
Churston Ferrers 88
W Looe
Yealmpton
79 Modbury
Moreleigh
Dartmouth
Kingswear
Polperro
Plymstock
Mount Edgcumbe 42
78 Ringmore
80 St Ann's Chapel
85 Slapton
Strete
Stoke Fleming
Kingsbridge
Bantham 81
82 Salcombe
Frogmore 83
Beesands 84
A39
A399
A361
B3223
A396
A373
A377
B3220
A386
A3072
A30
A3052
M5
A38
B3212
A382
A384
A380
A381
A390
A385
A379

MAP 2

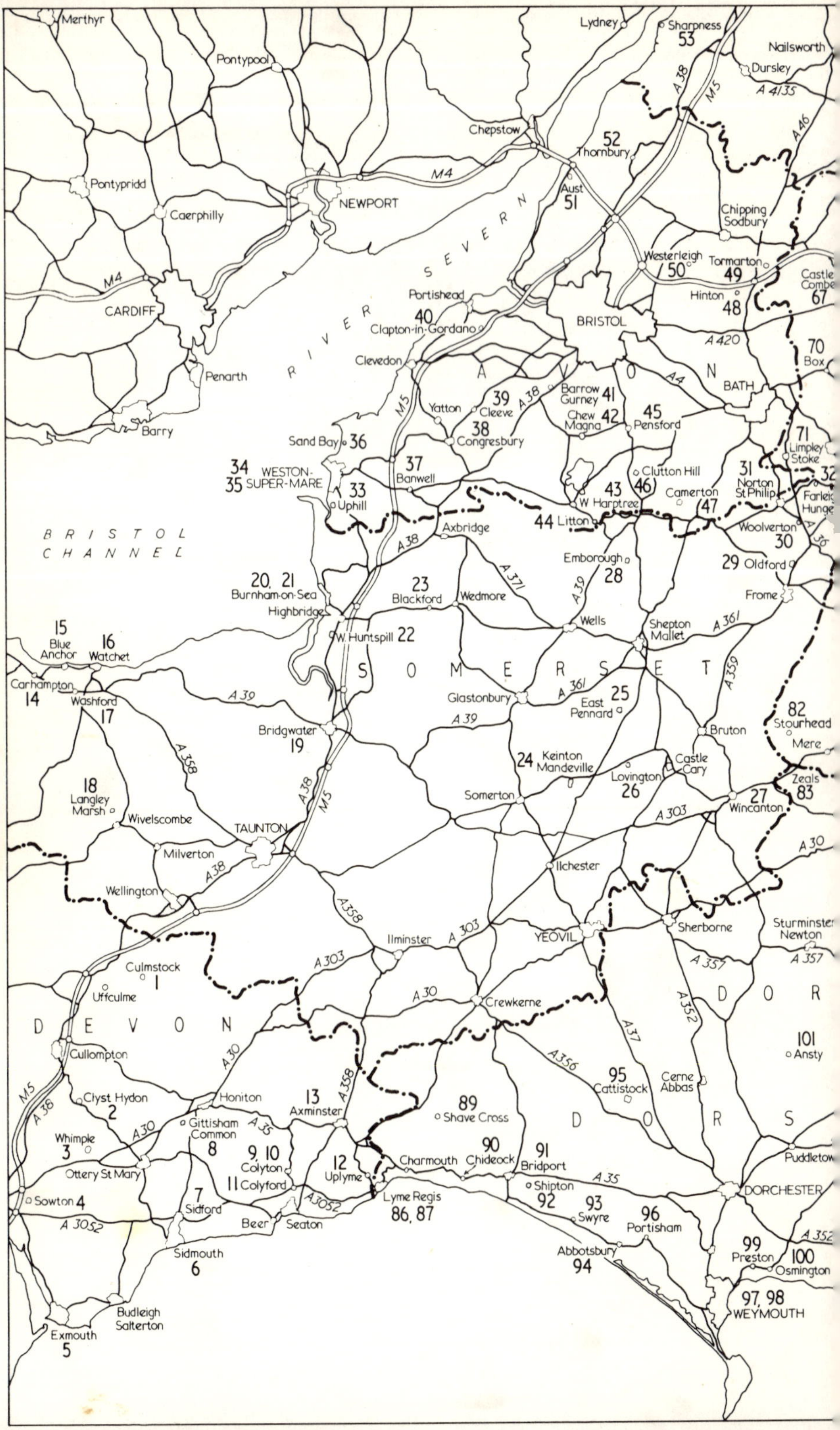
Merthyr
Pontypool
Lydney
Sharpness
53
Nailsworth
Dursley
A 4135
A 38
M5
A 46
Chepstow
52
Thornbury
M4
Pontypridd
NEWPORT
Aust
51
Caerphilly
RIVER SEVERN
Chipping Sodbury
Westerleigh
50
Tormarton
49
Castle Combe
67
M4
CARDIFF
Portishead
40
Clapton-in-Gordano
BRISTOL
Hinton
48
A 420
70
Box
Penarth
Clevedon
AVON
BATH
A4
Barry
Yatton
39
Cleeve
A 38
Barrow Gurney
41
Chew Magna
42
45
Pensford
38
Congresbury
71
Limpley Stoke
Sand Bay
36
37
Banwell
Clutton Hill
31
Norton St Philip
32
34
35
WESTON-SUPER-MARE
33
Uphill
43
W Harptree
46
Camerton
47
Farleigh Hungerford
44
Litton
Woolverton
30
BRISTOL CHANNEL
Axbridge
A 371
Emborough
28
29
Oldford
A 36
20, 21
Burnham-on-Sea
Highbridge
23
Blackford
Wedmore
A 39
Frome
Wells
Shepton Mallet
A 361
15
Blue Anchor
16
Watchet
W. Huntspill
22
SOMERSET
Carhampton
14
Washford
17
A 39
Glastonbury
A 361
East Pennard
25
A 359
82
Stourhead
Mere
Bridgwater
19
A 358
A 39
Bruton
18
Langley Marsh
Wivelscombe
24
Keinton Mandeville
Lovington
26
Castle Cary
Zeals
83
Somerton
27
Wincanton
A 303
TAUNTON
A 38
M5
Milverton
A 38
A 30
Wellington
Ilchester
A 358
Sturminster Newton
Ilminster
A 303
YEOVIL
Sherborne
A 303
A 357
A 357
Culmstock
1
Uffculme
A 30
Crewkerne
DORSET
DEVON
A 352
A 37
101
Ansty
A 356
Cullompton
A 30
95
Cattistock
Cerne Abbas
M5
A 38
Clyst Hydon
2
Honiton
13
Axminster
A 358
89
Shave Cross
Whimple
3
Gittisham Common
8
A 35
A 30
9, 10
Colyton
90
Chideock
91
Bridport
Puddletown
Ottery St Mary
12
Uplyme
Charmouth
11
Colyford
Shipton
92
A 35
DORCHESTER
Sowton
4
7
Sidford
A 3052
Lyme Regis
86, 87
93
Swyre
96
Portisham
A 3052
Beer
Seaton
A 352
Sidmouth
6
Abbotsbury
94
99
Preston
100
Osmington
97, 98
WEYMOUTH
Budleigh Salterton
Exmouth
5

MAP 2

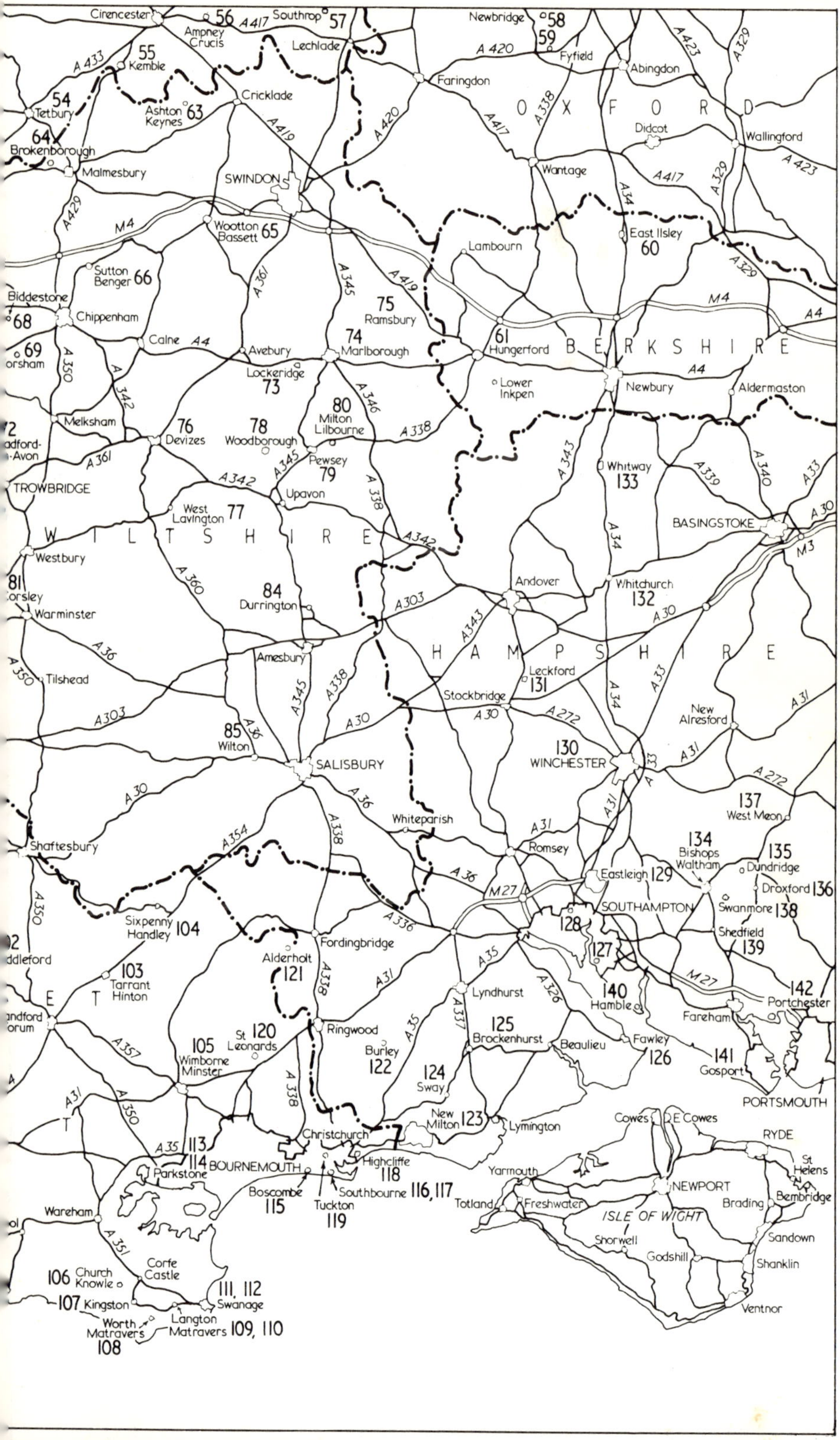

Cirencester
56 *A 417* Southrop 57
Ampney Crucis
Lechlade
Newbridge 58
59 Fyfield
Abingdon

55 Kemble
A 433
Ashton 63
Keynes
Cricklade
Faringdon
A 420
O X F O R D
A 423
A 429
A 329

54 Tetbury
64 Brokenborough
Malmesbury
A 429
A 419
SWINDON
Wantage
A 417
A 329
Didcot
Wallingford
A 423

68
69 orsham
Chippenham
Calne *A 4*
Avebury
61 Hungerford
B E R K S H I R E
A 4
Newbury
Aldermaston
M 4

Biddestone
Wootton 65
Bassett
Sutton 66
Benger
M 4
Lambourn
East Ilsley 60
A 34
M 4
A 4

A 361
75 Ramsbury
74 Marlborough
A 345
A 419
Lower 133 Whitway
Inkpen

76 Devizes
78 Woodborough
80 Milton
Lilbourne
79 Pewsey
Upavon
A 338
A 343
A 339
A 340
A 33

Melksham
adford-Avon
TROWBRIDGE
A 361
73 Lockeridge
A 346
A 342
A 345

W I L T S H I R E
81 West 77
Lavington
84 Durrington
A 342
132 Whitchurch
BASINGSTOKE
A 30
M 3

Westbury
orsley
Warminster
A 36
A 360
Amesbury
Andover
A 303
A 34
A 33

Tilshead
A 350
A 303
85 Wilton
A 345
A 338
A 30
H A M P S H I R E
Leckford 131
Stockbridge
A 30
A 272
New
Alresford
A 31

Shaftesbury
A 30
SALISBURY
A 36
Whiteparish
130 WINCHESTER
137 West Meon

A 350
A 354
A 338
Romsey
A 31
Eastleigh 129
134 Bishops
Waltham
135 Dundridge
Droxford 136

Sixpenny 104
Handley
Fordingbridge
A 336
A 36
M 27
SOUTHAMPTON
Swanmore 138
Shedfield 139

iddleford
103 Tarrant
Hinton
Alderholt 121
A 338
A 31
128 127
Lyndhurst
125 Brockenhurst
140 Hamble
142 Portchester
Fareham

andford
orum
105 St 120
Leonards
Wimborne
Minster
Ringwood
Burley 122
124 Sway
Beaulieu
Fawley 126
141 Gosport

A 357
A 35
A 337
A 326
M 27
PORTSMOUTH

Wareham
113
114
Parkstone
BOURNEMOUTH
Boscombe 115
Christchurch
Highcliffe 118
Southbourne 116, 117
Tuckton 119
New 123
Milton
Lymington
Yarmouth
Totland
Freshwater
Shorwell
Cowes E Cowes
NEWPORT
I S L E O F W I G H T
RYDE
St
Helens
Bembridge
Brading
Sandown
Shanklin

106 Church
Knowle
Corfe
Castle
111, 112 Swanage
107 Kingston
Worth
Matravers 109, 110
108
Godshill
Ventnor

MAP 3

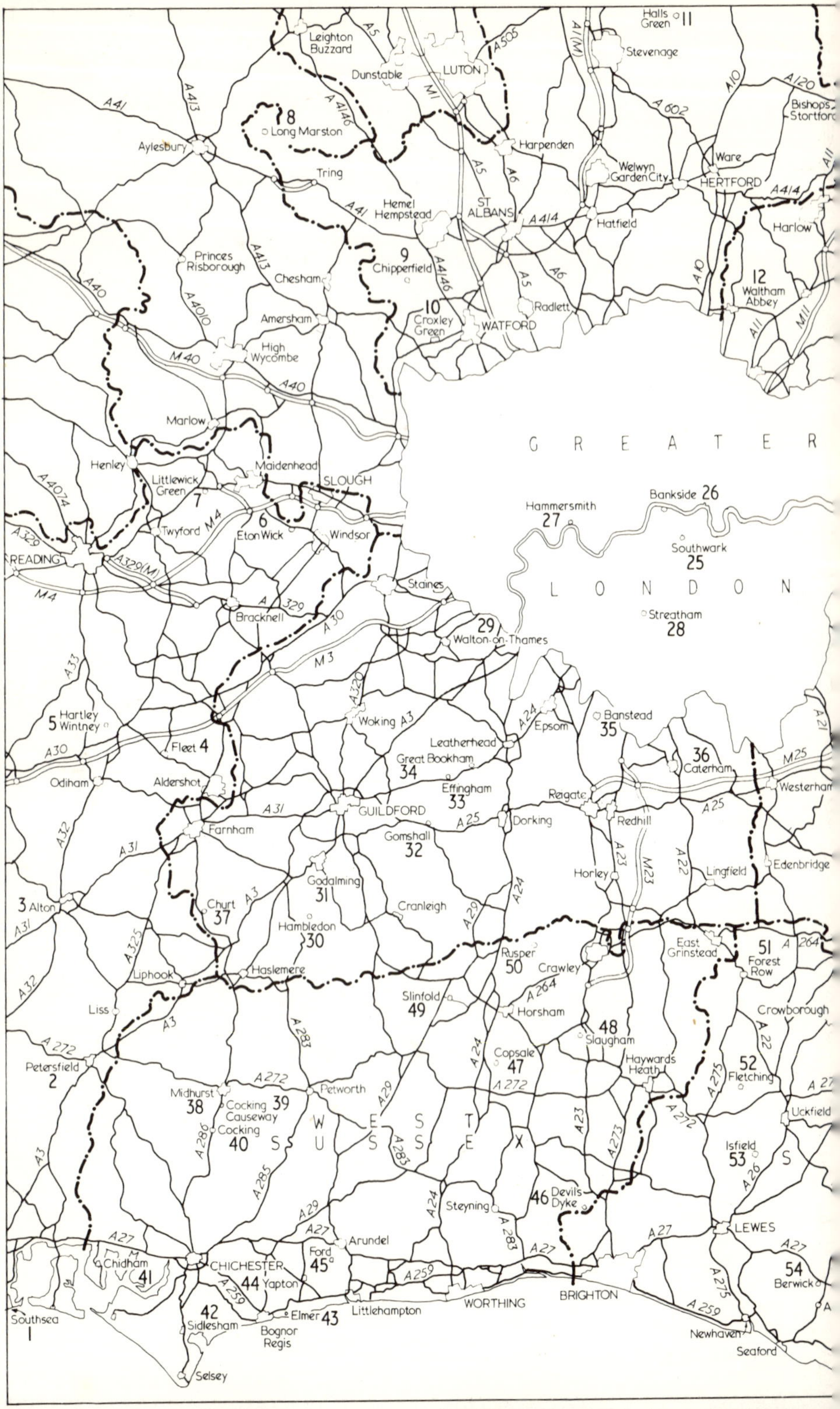

12

Halls Green 11
Leighton Buzzard
Dunstable
LUTON
Stevenage
Bishops Stortford
Long Marston 8
Harpenden
Welwyn Garden City
HERTFORD
Ware
Aylesbury
Tring
Hemel Hempstead
ST ALBANS
Hatfield
Harlow
Princes Risborough
Chesham
Chipperfield 9
Radlett
Waltham Abbey 12
Amersham
Croxley Green 10
WATFORD
High Wycombe
Marlow
Henley
Littlewick Green 7
Maidenhead
SLOUGH
G R E A T E R
Bankside 26
Hammersmith 27
Twyford
Eton Wick 6
Windsor
Southwark 25
READING
Bracknell
Staines
L O N D O N
Streatham 28
Walton-on-Thames 29
M3
Hartley Wintney 5
Woking A3
Leatherhead
Epsom
Banstead 35
36 Caterham
M25
Westerham
Fleet 4
Great Bookham 34
Effingham 33
Aldershot
GUILDFORD
Dorking
Reigate
Redhill
Edenbridge
Odiham
Farnham
Gomshall 32
Horley
Lingfield
Alton 3
Godalming 31
Cranleigh
East Grinstead
Forest Row 51
Churt 37
Hambledon 30
Rusper 50
Crawley
Liphook
Haslemere
Crowborough
Liss
Slinfold 49
Horsham
Fletching 52
Petersfield 2
Midhurst 38
Petworth
Copsale 47
Slaugham 48
Haywards Heath
Uckfield
Cocking Causeway 39
Cocking 40
W E S T   S U S S E X
Isfield 53
Chidham 41
CHICHESTER
Yapton 44
Ford 45
Arundel
Devils Dyke 46
Steyning
LEWES
Berwick 54
Southsea 1
Sidlesham 42
Bognor Regis
Elmer 43
Littlehampton
WORTHING
BRIGHTON
Newhaven
Seaford
Selsey

MAP 3

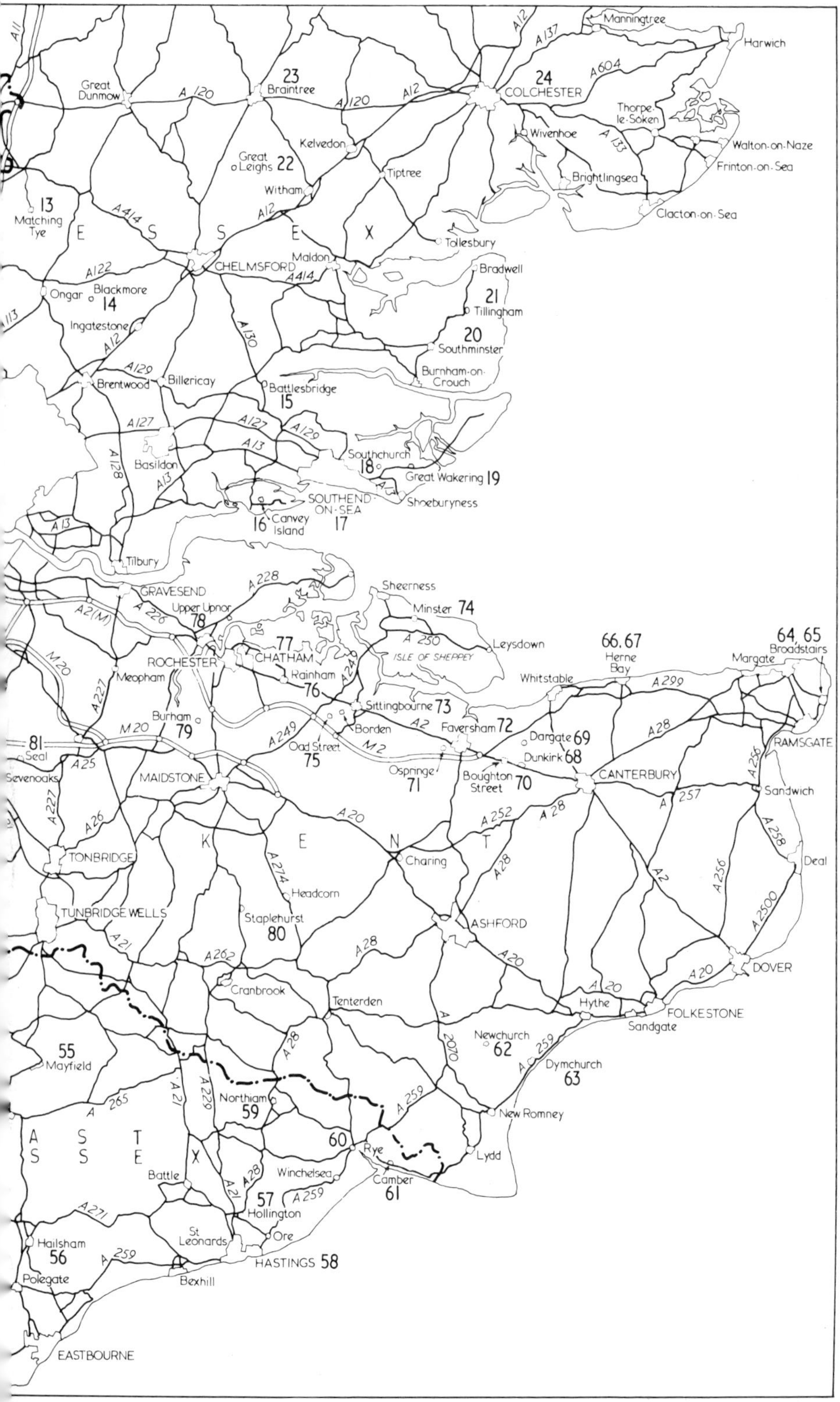

Manningtree

A137 A12

Harwich

A120 23 Braintree A120 A12 24 COLCHESTER A604

Great Dunmow

Kelvedon

Thorpe le-Soken

Walton-on-Naze

Wivenhoe

13 Matching Tye

E S S E X

Great 22 o Leighs

Witham

Tiptree

A12 A133

Brightlingsea

Frinton-on-Sea

A414

A12

Tollesbury

Clacton-on-Sea

A122

CHELMSFORD A414

Maldon

Bradwell

Ongar o Blackmore 14

A130

21 Tillingham

Ingatestone A12

20 Southminster

A129

Brentwood Billericay

Battlesbridge 15

Burnham-on-Crouch

A128 A127 A127 A13 A129

Basildon A13

Southchurch 18 o Great Wakering 19

A13 Tilbury

SOUTHEND-ON-SEA

16 Canvey island 17 Shoeburyness

A228

GRAVESEND Upper Upnor

Sheerness

Minster 74

A2(M) A226

78

ISLE OF SHEPPEY

Leysdown

66, 67 Herne Bay

64, 65 Broadstairs

M20 ROCHESTER 77 CHATHAM

A250

Whitstable

Margate

A227 Meopham

Rainham 76 A2

Sittingbourne 73 Faversham 72

A299 A28

RAMSGATE

M20 Burham 79

A249 Oad Street 75

Borden A2 Dargate 69 Dunkirk 68

A28

81 Seal

A25

MAIDSTONE

Ospringe 71 Boughton Street 70

CANTERBURY

A257

Sandwich

A258

Sevenoaks A227

A26

A20

A252 A28

A2 A256

Deal

TONBRIDGE

K E N T

Charing

A28

A2500

TUNBRIDGE WELLS

A21 A274 Headcorn

ASHFORD

A20

DOVER

A262 Staplehurst 80

A28

Hythe

A20 A20

55 Mayfield

Cranbrook

Tenterden

Newchurch 62 A259

FOLKESTONE Sandgate

A265 A21 A229 Northiam 59

A28 A259

Dymchurch 63

E A S T S U S S E X

60 Rye

New Romney

A271 Battle

A28 A21 Winchelsea 57 Hollington

A259 Camber 61

Lydd

56 Hailsham A259

St Leonards Ore

Polegate Bexhill

HASTINGS 58

EASTBOURNE

MAP 4

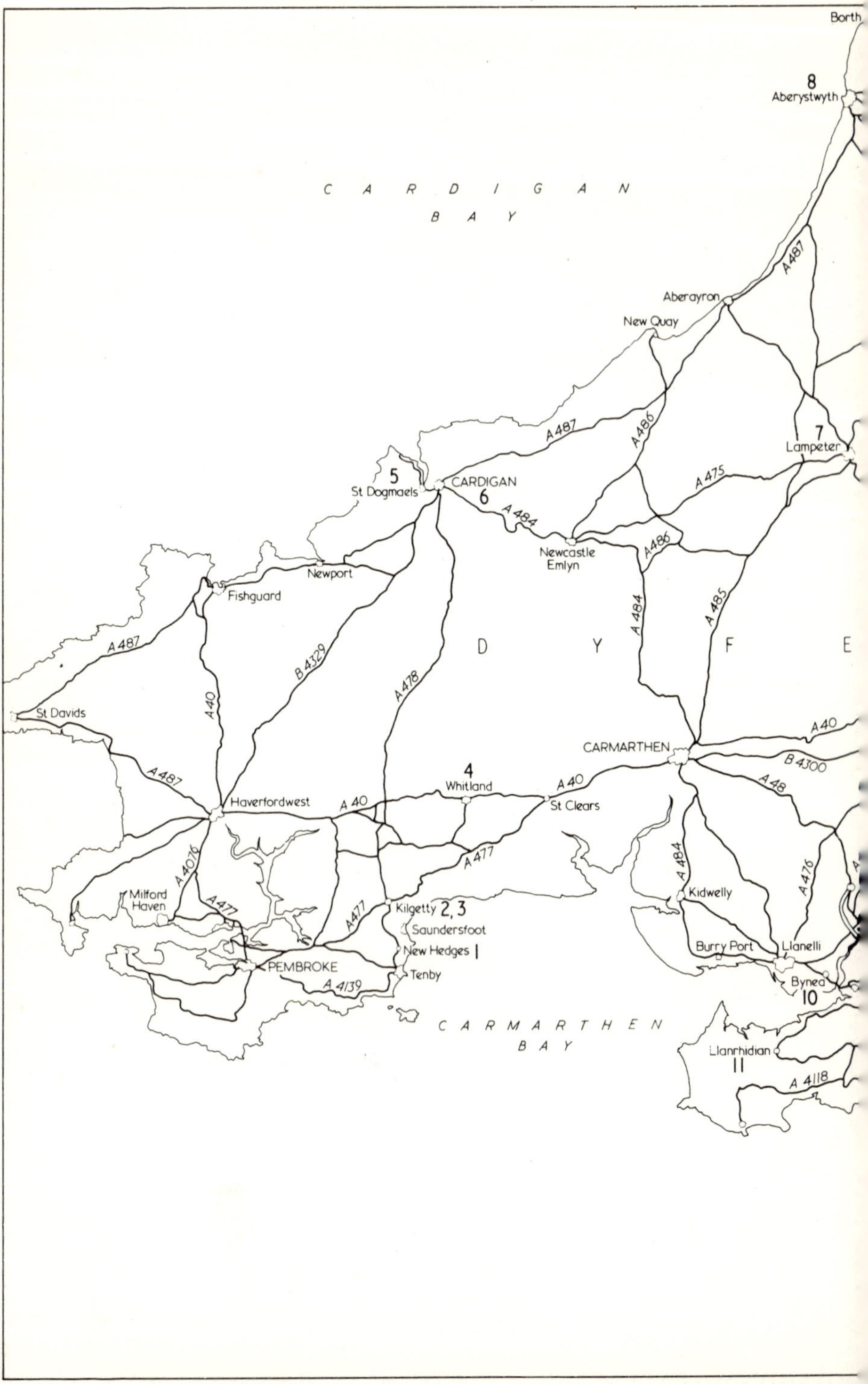

14

MAP 4

Borth

8
Aberystwyth

C A R D I G A N
B A Y

A487

Aberayron

New Quay

A486

A487

7
Lampeter

A475

5
St Dogmaels

CARDIGAN

6

A484

Newcastle
Emlyn

A486

A485

Newport

A484

Fishguard

D   Y   F   E

A487

B4329

A478

St Davids

A40

CARMARTHEN

A40

B4300

Haverfordwest

A40

Whitland

4

A40

St Clears

A48

A477

A484

A476

A4076

A477

Milford
Haven

Kidwelly

A477

Kilgetty 2, 3

Saundersfoot

Burry Port

Llanelli

New Hedges 1

PEMBROKE

A4139

Tenby

Bynea

10

C A R M A R T H E N
B A Y

Llanrhidian

11

A4118

MAP 4

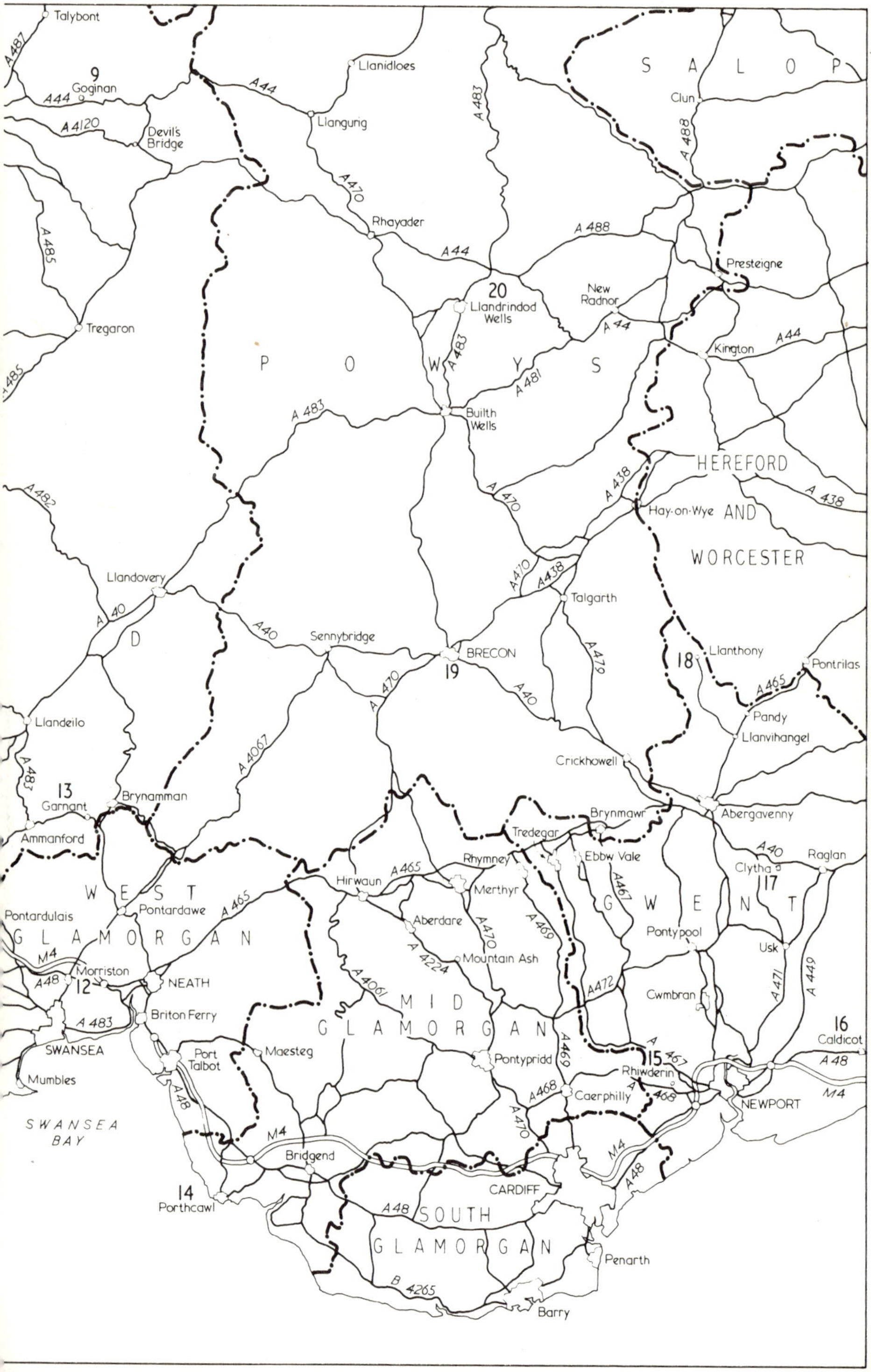

Talybont
A487
9
Goginan
A44
A4120
Devil's Bridge
Llanidloes
Llangurig
A44
A483
S A L O P
Clun
A 488
A470
Rhayader
A 485
A44
A 488
Presteigne
20
Llandrindod Wells
New Radnor
A44
Tregaron
A485
P O W Y S
A483
A481
Kington
A44
Builth Wells
A 483
HEREFORD
A 482
A 470
A 438
Hay-on-Wye
AND
A 438
WORCESTER
Llandovery
A470
A438
Talgarth
A 40
D
A40
Sennybridge
BRECON
19
A479
18
Llanthony
Pontrilas
A 465
Pandy
Llanvihangel
A470
A40
Llandeilo
A 4067
Crickhowell
A 483
13
Garnant
Brynamman
Brynmawr
Abergavenny
Ammanford
Tredegar
Rhymney
Ebbw Vale
A40
Raglan
Hirwaun
A465
Merthyr
A461
Clytha
17
W E S T
Pontardawe
A 465
Aberdare
A470
A469
G W E N T
Pontardulais
G L A M O R G A N
Pontypool
Usk
M4
Morriston
A 4224
Mountain Ash
A48
12
NEATH
A4061
A472
Cwmbran
A471
A 449
Briton Ferry
M I D
A 483
G L A M O R G A N
16
Caldicot
SWANSEA
Port Talbot
Maesteg
Pontypridd
A469
15
A 467
Rhiwderin
A 48
Mumbles
A48
A468
Caerphilly
A 468
NEWPORT
M4
SWANSEA BAY
A470
M4
M4
Bridgend
A48
14
Porthcawl
CARDIFF
A48
SOUTH
GLAMORGAN
Penarth
B 4265
Barry

MAP 5

Market Drayton
Stone
Ellesmere 49
Oswestry
Wem
S T A F F O R
STAFFORD
51 Great Haywood
Rugeley
Newport
Longdon-upon-Tern 48
47 Oakengates
SHREWSBURY
Wellington
50 Wimblebur
Cannock
S A L O P
M54
26 Wednesfield
Willenhall 27
WOLVERHAMPTON
WALS 25
Much Wenlock
Darlaston 28
Montgomery
Church Stretton
Wentnor 45
Bridgnorth 46
44 Bishop's Castle
29
30 Brierley Hill
BIRMI
Clun
43 Cleobury Mortimer
Bewdley
Kidderminster
Ludlow
40 Newnham Bridge
Callow Hill 42
Knighton
39 Tenbury Wells
Stourport
Redditch
Brimfield 38
Lindridge 41
Droitwich
Leominster
Kington
WORCESTER
Bromyard
Weobley
H E R E F O R D A N D W O R C E S T E R
Great Malvern
Pershore
37 Hardwick
Evesham
Hay-on-Wye
Dorstone 36
HEREFORD
35 Peterchurch
Ledbury
Fownhope 31
G L O U C E S T
Newent
Ross-on-Wye 32
CHELTENHAM
33 Walford
Crickhowell
34 Symonds Yat
GLOUCESTER
6 Colesbourne
7 Chedworth
Cinderford
Abergavenny
Monmouth
G W E N T
Coleford 1, 2
Saul 3
Upper Framilode 4
5 Beechpike
Stroud
A5
A528
A49
A53
A519
A51
M6
A458
A488
A464
A442
A454
A489
A448
A441
A38
M5
A44
A422
A417
A4103
A480
A438
A449
A435
A465
M50
A40
A46
A48

D E R B Y

D

Uttoxeter
A50
Egginton 53
A6
Stretton 52
BURTON-ON-TRENT
A515
A38
A50
Ashby
Lichfield
A51
Long Clawson 63
Nether Broughton
A606
Melton Mowbray
A607
Loughborough
Whitwick 58
Quom 61
Barrow-on-Soar 62
A6
Copt Oak 59
Cropston 60
Syston 64 65
A607
A50
Heather 57
L E I C E S T E R
Tamworth
Twycross 56
Sheepy Magna 54
Pinwall 55
Atherstone
A5
Kingsbury 24
A47
Barwell
A447
67
A47
A46
LEICESTER 66
A47
Oakham
Uppingham
A6
Hinckley
A69
Nuneaton
A444
Frolesworth 68
A50
Market Harborough
Corby
A427
Coleshill
M6
A46
Ullesthorpe 69
Walcote 70
A427
Husbands Bosworth 71
A6
Kettering
HAM
A45
M42
COVENTRY
A427
A45
Rugby
Hillmorton 23
22
Clay Coton
Crick
Welford 21
West Haddon
A50
A508
A443
M41
Kenilworth
A445
M45
A5
A428
Wellingborough
Leamington Spa
A423
NORTHAMPTON
Warwick
A46
W A R W I C K
A425
Daventry
A45
NORTHAMPTON
A428
Southam
20 Weedon Beck
A45
A43
M1
Olney
Alcester
A422
A439
A41
Stratford-on-Avon
Farthingstone 19
Towcester
Weston 18
A422
A429
Little Bourton 12
Banbury
Cosgrove 17
A5
Broadway
Chipping Campden 10
Epwell 11
A34
A424
A43
Brackley
Buckingham
Bletchley
A421
Moreton-in-Marsh
A361
Adderbury 13
Aynho 14
A413
Leighton Buzzard
R
Stow-on-the-Wold 9
A44
Chipping Norton
A423
A41
A421
A436
A429
A361
A34
Wootton 15
Bicester
B U C K I N G H A M
A41
Northleach
O X F O R D
Woodstock
A34
Aylesbury
A41
A40
Burford
Witney 16
OXFORD
Thame
A433
Bibury 8
A40

MAP 6

18

Navenby

Tattershall

Stickney

Sibsey

A52 Skegness **48**

47 Wainfleet

A15 A17 A153 A155 A16

Sleaford

A153 A17 A52 A16 A52

31 Thornham

Hunstanton

Docking

GRANTHAM

A52

L I N C O L N

Kirton

46 Sutterton

T H E   W A S H

A149

A1

Pinchbeck **44**

Bourne

A151 A15 A151 A151

Spalding

Holbeach **45**

Long Sutton

A17

32 North Wootton

KINGS LYNN

A17

Gayton **33**

N

Essendine

43 Barholm

A16

Crowland

A47 Thorney

Guyhirne

A1101 A47 A10 A10

Wisbech

Downham Market

Hilgay

A134 Stoke Ferry

Ketton

Stamford

A1 A15

Castor

PETERBOROUGH

Whittlesey

A1141

March

A101

Weldon

Oundle

Stilton

Ramsey

Chatteris

A142

Littleport

ELY

22 West Row

A1101

A142

Mildenhall

42 Thorpe Waterville

Thrapston

C A M B R I D G E

Sutton

Freckenham **21**

A604

Alconbury

A141

Earith

A1123

Soham

A10

A6 45 A

Rushden

41 Tilbrook

Kimbolton

1 Upper Dean

HUNTINGDON

A45 A1

Cottenham

A10 **37** Waterbeach

38 Lode

39 Bottisham

Newmarket

A11

40 St Neots

A45

A604

CAMBRIDGE

A14

2 Roxton

Tempsford

3 Sandy

Potton **4**

A608

Harston

A10

A130

Linton A604

Hundon **11**

10 Haverhill

Turvey A428

BEDFORD

Melbourn

A505

A422 A6

B E D F O R D

A5140 A418 A600 A6

Biggleswade

Ampthill

Shefford

A507

A1

Hinxworth

5

Royston

A505

M11

Saffron Walden

A130 Finchingfield

A507 Baldock

6

Weston

A507

Chipping **8**

A10

Newport

E Thaxted

S

Great Bardfield

9

M1

A507 A6

Letchworth

Hitchin

A505

Buntingford

N O R T H   S E A

Wells
A149
Sheringham
A149
Cromer
A148
Holt
Mundesley
North Creake
Little Walsingham
South Creake
30
Fakenham
A148
Melton Constable
A140
A149
North Walsham
Palling **27**
Stalham
Wayfordbridge
28
Aylsham
29
Cawston
Coltishead
A149
Castle Acre
34
East Dereham
A1067
A47
N O R F O L K
NORWICH
A47
Acle
A47
Caister-on-Sea
GREAT YARMOUTH
Gorleston
Swaffham
A1075
Brundall
26
Watton
A1151
A146
Reedham Ferry
25
Hilborough
35
Wymondham
A11
Loddon
Burgh St Peter
24
LOWESTOFT
Thompson
36
Attleborough
A140
Tivetshall
Bungay **17**
Harleston
A143
Beccles
A146
Brandon
A1065
A134
A1075
Thetford
A1066
Diss
Brockdish
23
Wingfield
19
Huntingfield
Halesworth
18
A144
A145
A12
Wrentham
Southwold
Walberswick
A11
A1101
A143
Walsham-le-Willows
20
A140
A1120
A12
BURY ST EDMUNDS
S U F F O L K
Debenham
Framlingham
Saxmundham
Leiston
143
A134
Stowmarket
A1120
Wickham Market
Snape
Aldeburgh
A45
Needham Market
A45
A12
Lavenham
14
Naughton
Claydon
Woodbridge
Cavendish
12
Long Melford
13
Whatfield **15**
IPSWICH
Clare
Sudbury
A1071
Hadleigh
A45
Pin Mill **16**
A13
Bures
A12
A137
Felixstowe
E
X
A134
Halstead
A604
Harwich
A604

MAP 7

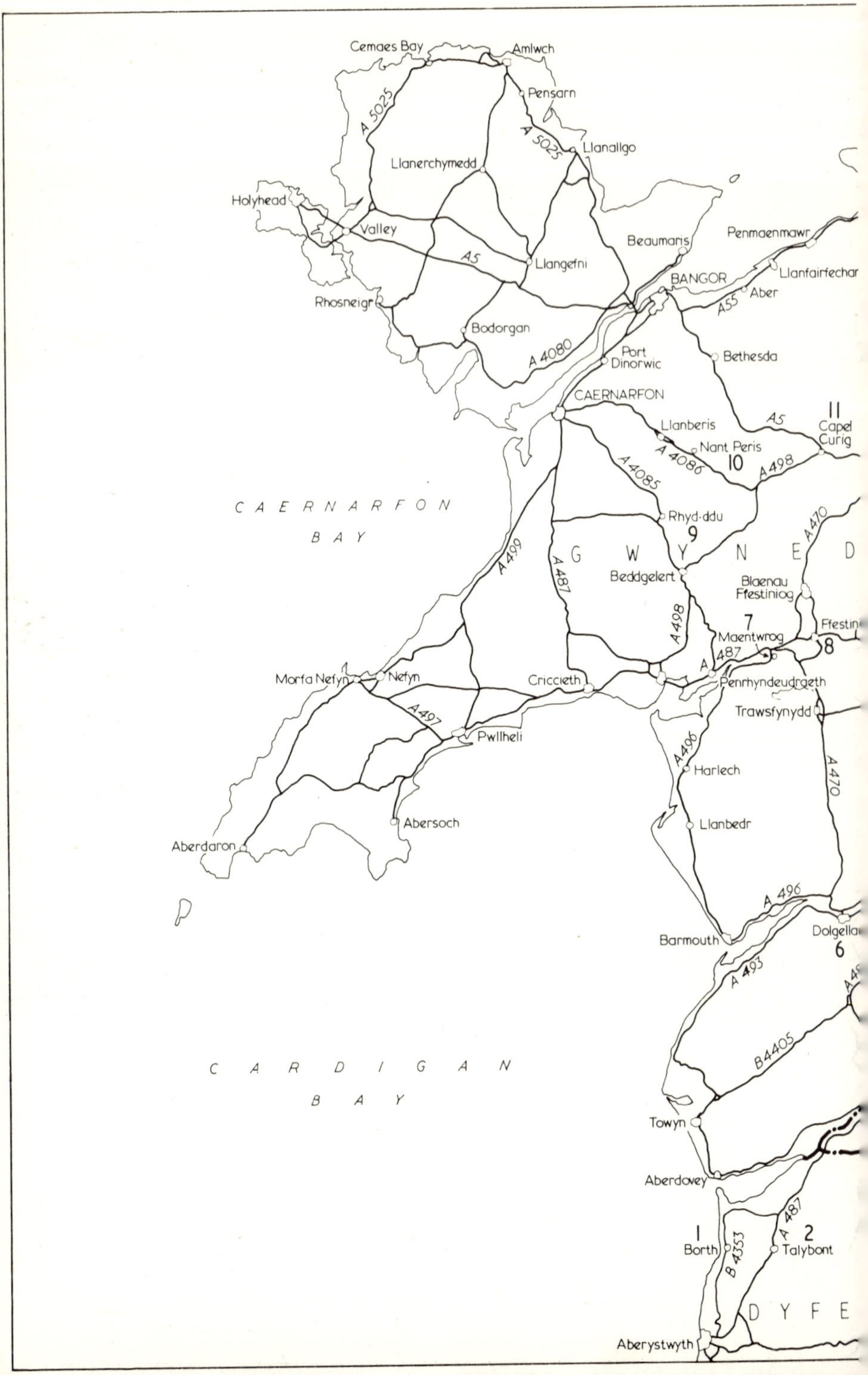

20

Cemaes Bay
Amlwch
Pensarn
A 5025
A 5025
Llanallgo
Llanerchymedd
Holyhead
Valley
A 5
Llangefni
Beaumaris
Penmaenmawr
BANGOR
Llanfairfechan
A55
Aber
Rhosneigr
Bodorgan
A 4080
Port Dinorwic
Bethesda
CAERNARFON
Llanberis
A 5
11
Nant Peris
Capel Curig
A 4086
10
A 498
CAERNARFON BAY
A 4085
Rhyd-ddu
9
A 499
G W Y N E D D
Beddgelert
Blaenau Ffestiniog
A 498
7
Ffestin
Maentwrog
8
A 487
Morfa Nefyn
Nefyn
Criccieth
Penrhyndeudraeth
A 497
Trawsfynydd
Pwllheli
A 496
Harlech
Abersoch
A 470
Llanbedr
Aberdaron
A 496
CARDIGAN BAY
Barmouth
Dolgella
A 495
6
B 4405
Towyn
A 470
Aberdovey
1
A 487
2
Borth
B 4353
Talybont
D Y F E
Aberystwyth

LIVERPOOL

Hoylake

West Kirby

BIRKENHEAD

M 62

Heswall

R. Dee

M 53

R Mersey

Neston

Ellesmere Port

M 56

Llandudno

14

Rhyl

Prestatyn

Colwyn Bay

A 548

A 5151

A 41

A 540

A 56

Conwy

A 55

Abergele

13

A 55

Holywell

Flint

A 548

CHESTER

A 51

St Asaph

A 548

A 541

A 55

A 548

A 549

A 483

Denbigh

A 544

A 525

Mold

A 541

Llanrwst

C L W Y D

A 543

Ruthin

15

A 534

A 41

A 470

12

Betws-y-Coed

B 5105

Graigfechan

16

A 525

WREXHAM

A 5106

D

A 5

A 494

A 5104

17

Gyfelia

A 525

Whitchurch

A 4212

Corwen

A 5

Ruabon

Cynwyd

18

Llangollen

A 494

Bala

Pontfadog

19

Chirk

Ellesmere

Glyn Ceiriog

A 483

Oswestry

Wem

A 470

B 4391

B 5480

A 528

A 49

A 494

Llanfyllin

A 5

SHREWSBURY

A 470

A 458

A 495

A 490

A 483

A 458

Llangadfan

5

Welshpool

S A L O P

Llanfair Caereinion

4

A 458

Machynlleth

A 470

P O W Y S

Montgomery

A 490

Church Stretton

Newtown

A 489

Bishops Castle

3

Llandinam

A 492

A 483

Llanidloes

Clun

MAP 8

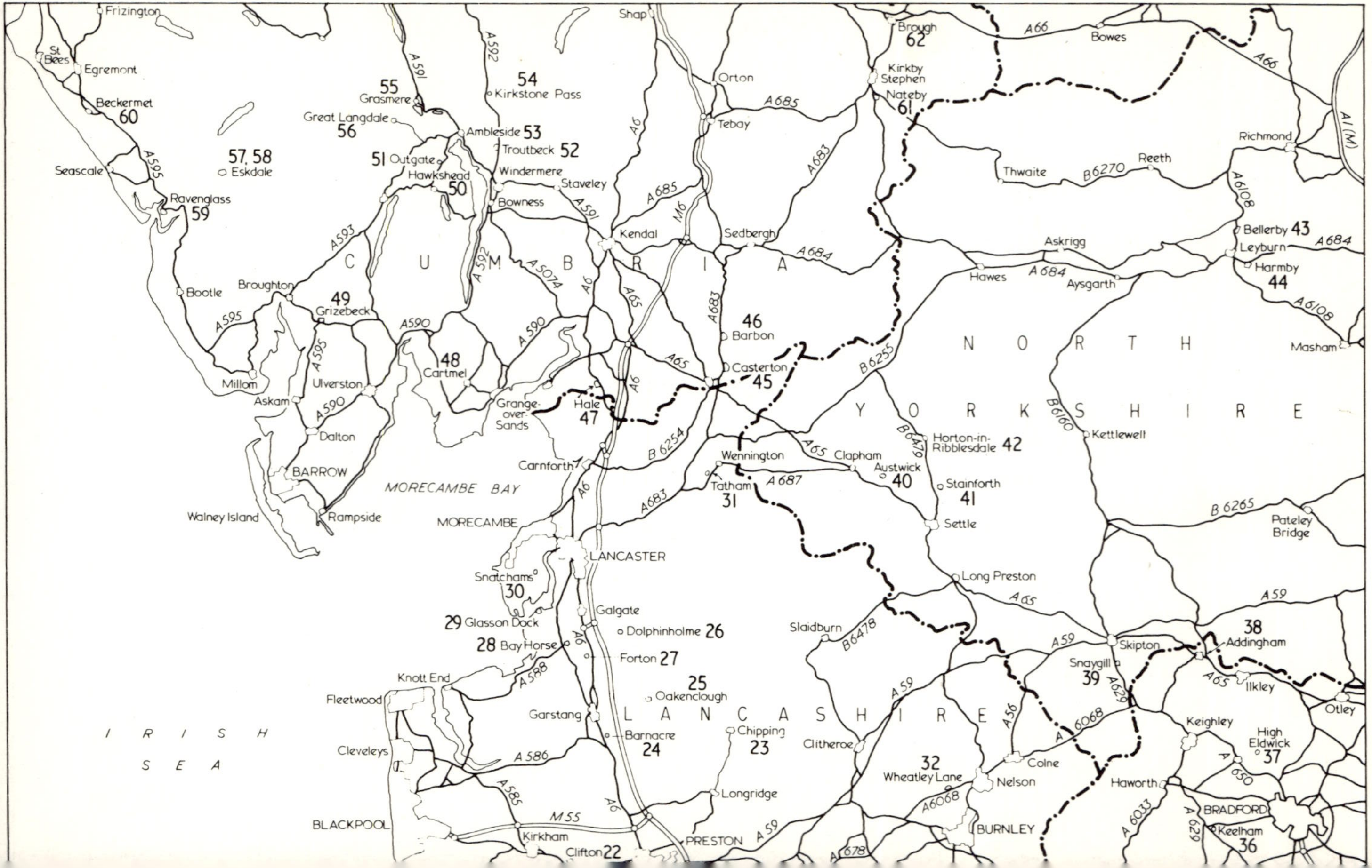

Frizington
St Bees
Egremont
Beckermet
60
Seascale
Ravenglass
59
57, 58
Eskdale
Bootle
Millom
Askam
Broughton
49
Grizebeck
Ulverston
Dalton
BARROW
Walney Island
Rampside
55
Grasmere
Great Langdale
56
51
Outgate
Hawkshead
50
Ambleside 53
54
Kirkstone Pass
Troutbeck 52
Windermere
Bowness
Staveley
Shap
Kendal
48
Cartmel
Grange-over-Sands
Hale
47
Carnforth
MORECAMBE BAY
MORECAMBE
LANCASTER
Snatchams
30
29 Glasson Dock
28 Bay Horse
Galgate
Dolphinholme 26
Forton 27
25
Oakenclough
Knott End
Fleetwood
Cleveleys
BLACKPOOL
Garstang
Barnacre
24
Chipping
23
Longridge
Kirkham
Clifton 22
PRESTON
IRISH SEA
CUMBRIA
LANCASHIRE
NORTH YORKSHIRE
Orton
Tebay
Sedbergh
46
Barbon
Casterton
45
Wennington
Tatham
31
Clapham
Austwick
40
Horton-in-Ribblesdale 42
Stainforth
41
Settle
Long Preston
Slaidburn
Clitheroe
32
Wheatley Lane
Nelson
Colne
BURNLEY
Snaygill
39
Skipton
38
Addingham
Ilkley
Otley
Keighley
High Eldwick
37
Haworth
BRADFORD
Keelham
36
Brough
62
Kirkby Stephen
Nateby
61
Bowes
Richmond
Thwaite
Reeth
Askrigg
Hawes
Aysgarth
Bellerby 43
Leyburn
Harmby
44
Masham
Kettlewell
Pateley Bridge
A1(M)
A66
A685
A683
A6
A592
A591
A595
A593
A5074
A590
A65
M6
A684
A6108
B6270
B6255
B6160
B6479
B6254
A687
B6478
B6265
A59
A56
A629
A6068
A650
A6033
A678
A588
A586
A585
M55

MAP 8

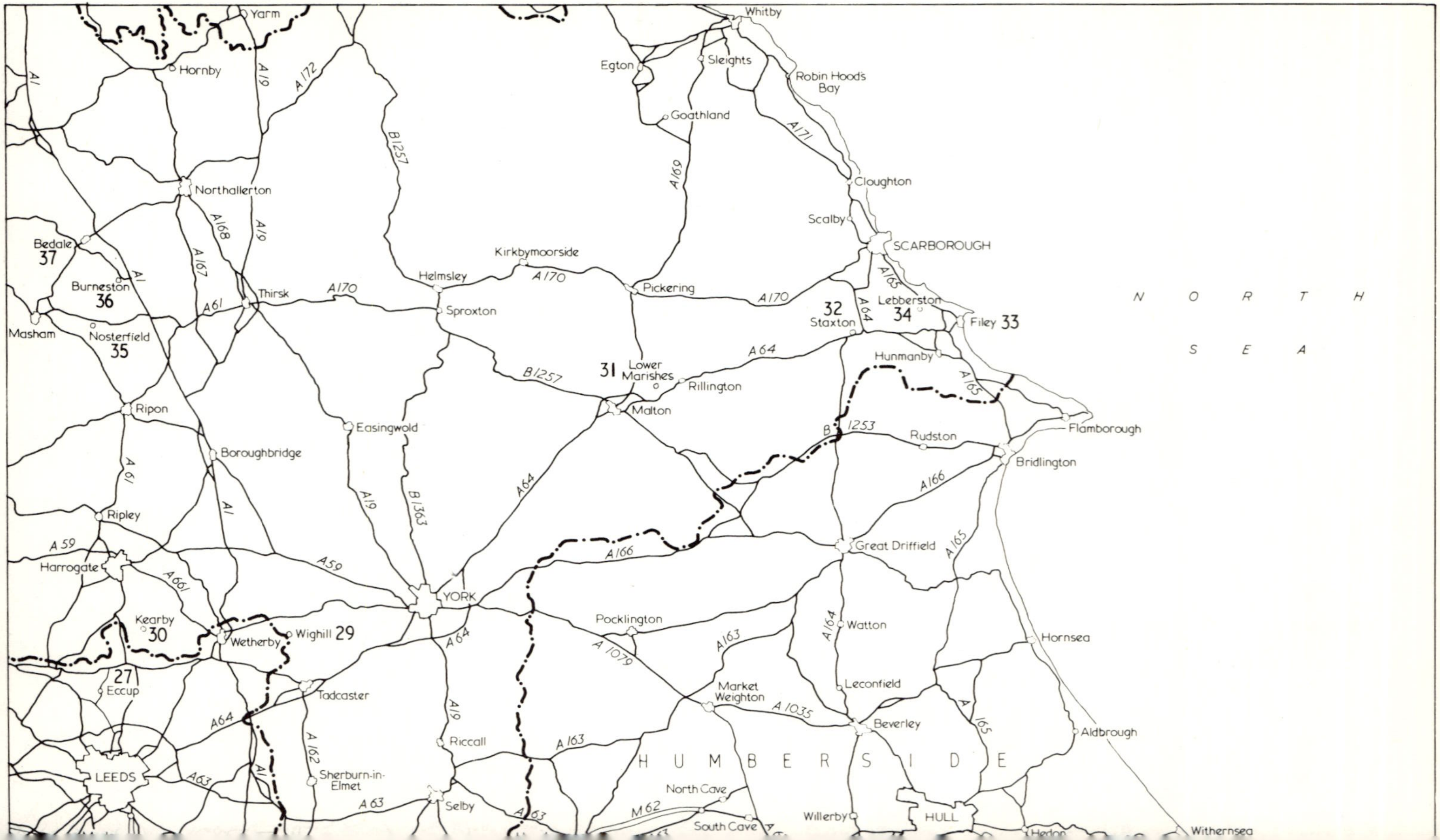

MAP 9

24

NORTH SEA

Withernsea
Hornsea
Aldbrough
Bridlington
Flamborough
Rudston
Hunmanby
Filey 33
Lebberston 34
SCARBOROUGH
Cloughton
Scalby
Robin Hood's Bay
Staxton 32
A64
A165
A166
A614
A165
HULL
Willerby
Beverley
Leconfield
Watton
Great Driffield
A164
A1035
Market Weighton
South Cave
North Cave
HUMBERSIDE
M62
A63
A1079
A163
Pocklington
A166
A163
Selby
Riccall
A19
B1253
B1257
Rillington
Malton
Lower Marishes 31
Pickering
Kirkbymoorside
A170
A169
Goathland
Egton
Sleights
Whitby
A171
A172
Yarm
Hornby
A19
Northallerton
A168
A167
Thirsk
A61
A170
Sproxton
Helmsley
B1257
Easingwold
B1363
A19
YORK
A64
A59
Boroughbridge
A1
Ripon
A61
Nosterfield 35
Masham
Burneston 36
Bedale 37
A1
Ripley
Harrogate
A59
A661
Kearby 30
Wetherby
Wighill 29
Tadcaster
Sherburn-in-Elmet
A162
A1
A64
A63
Eccup 27
LEEDS

DEWSBURY
WAKEFIELD
Whitwood 26
Carlton 28
Goole
Hessle
New Holland
Barton on-Humber
South Ferriby
HUMBER
Patrington
Easington
Rawcliffe
23
Thorne
Crowle
Scunthorpe
Ulceby
Immingham
GRIMSBY
Cleethorpes
Cudworth
BARNSLEY
24
Hatfield Woodhouse
22
Belton
Epworth
Brigg
Wrawby
Laceby
DONCASTER
Penistone
Mexborough
21
Westwoodside
Haxey
Kirton-in-Lindsey
Caister
North Coates
North Somercotes
Saltfleet
ROTHERHAM
Tickhill
Maltby
Bawtry
Blyton
Binbrook
25
Hollow Meadows
SHEFFIELD
Gainsborough
Market Rasen
Louth
Bamford 1
Blyth
11
Worksop
Retford
19. 20
Mablethorpe
Withern
Sutton-on-Sea
L I N C O L N
12
Torksey
13
Saxilby
Wragby
Alford
18
Huttoft
16
Chapel St Leonards
CHESTERFIELD
Tuxford
LINCOLN
14
Washingborough
Bardney
Horncastle
17
Hogsthorpe
15
Ingoldmells
Bakewell
2
Rowsley
Scarcliffe
7
Ollerton
Spilsby
Skegness
3
Wensley
Clay Cross
4
Matlock
Mansfield
Woodhall Spa
5
Grange Mill
Kirkby-in Ashfield
Sutton-in Ashfield
Navenby
Nocton
Tattershall
Coningsby
Wainfleet
Wirksworth
Alfreton
Southwell
10
Newark on-Trent
6
Broadholme
Ripley
Belper
Hucknall
N O T T I N G H A M
Heanor
West Hallam 8
Nuthall 9
NOTTINGHAM
Long Bennington
Sleaford
Boston
M1
M18
A1(M)
M62
M180
A1
A6
A15
A16
A17
A18
A19
A46
A52
A57
A60
A61
A153
A156
A157
A158
A159
A617
A614
A616
A619
A620
A621
A629
A631
A635
A638
A1031
A1033
B1200
B1203
B1205

MAP 9

MAP 10

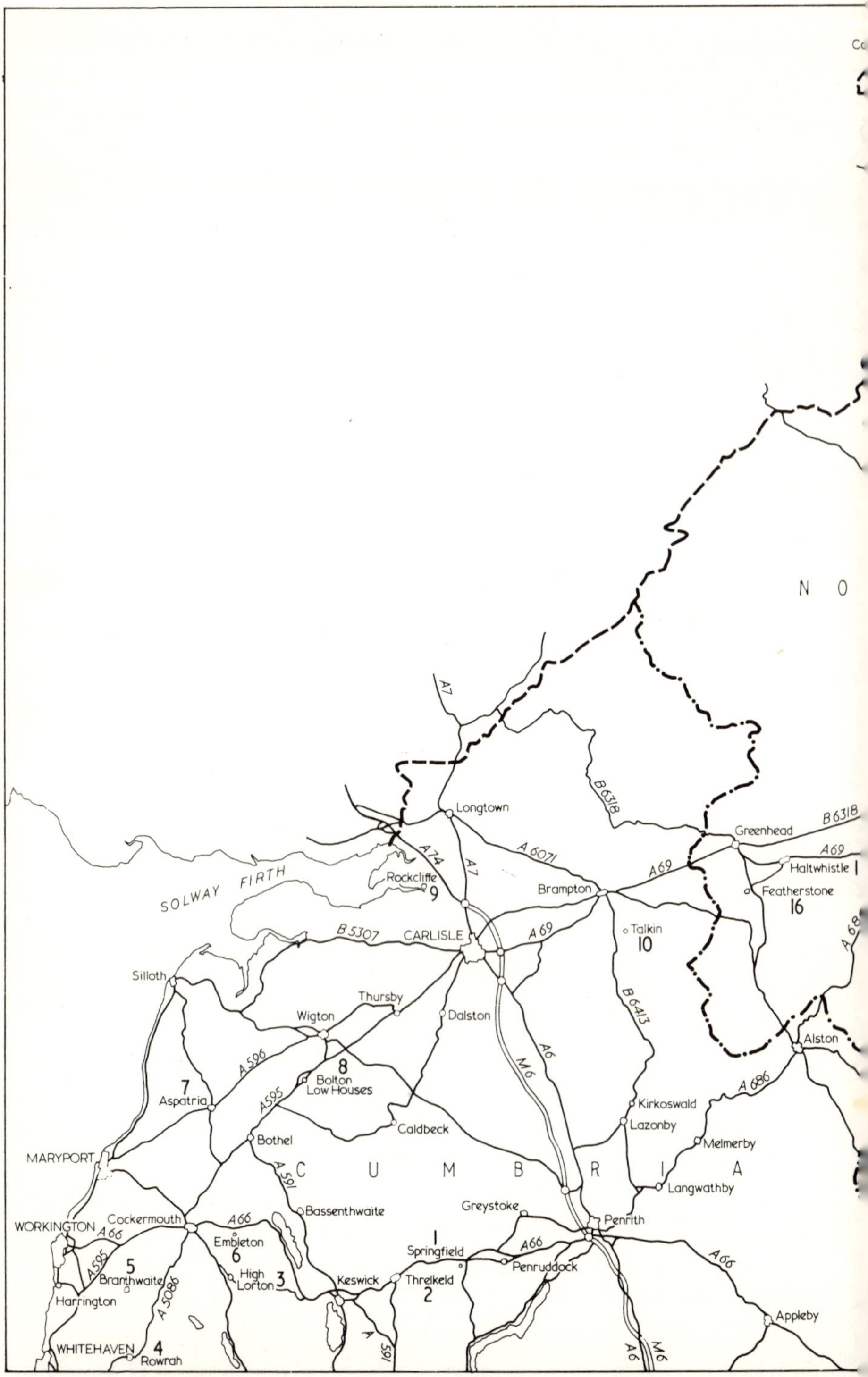

26

MAP 10

NO

Carlisle

Longtown

A7

A6071

B6318

Greenhead

B6318

A74

A7

A69

Haltwhistle

Rockcliffe

9

Brampton

Featherstone

16

SOLWAY FIRTH

B5307

CARLISLE

A69

Talkin

10

Silloth

A6

B6413

Wigton

Thursby

Dalston

Alston

M6

A686

Bolton Low Houses

8

A596

7

Aspatria

A595

Bothel

Caldbeck

Kirkoswald

Lazonby

Melmerby

MARYPORT

C U M B R I A

Langwathby

A591

WORKINGTON

Cockermouth

A66

Bassenthwaite

Greystoke

Penrith

A66

A66

A596

5

Branthwaite

Embleton

6

Springfield

1

A66

Penruddock

Harrington

A5086

High Lorton

3

Keswick

Threlkeld

2

Appleby

WHITEHAVEN

4

Rowrah

A591

A6

M6

MAP 10

Belford
Kirk Yetholme
Wooler
A 697
A 698
A1
Alnwick
Alnmouth
Amble
Rothbury
Felton
A 697
A 1068
18
Forestburn Gate
Longhorsley
Otterburn
N O R T H
S E A
THUMBERLAND
Ashington
Newbiggin-by-the-Sea
Morpeth
Bellingham
A 189
A 68
A 696
Blyth
Wark
Ponteland
NEWCASTLE
B 6318
SOUTH SHIELDS
A 69
Hexham
Corbridge
14
15
GATESHEAD
SUNDERLAND
A 19
Allendale Town
White-le-Head
13
Stanley
Consett
Chester-le-Street
Edmondsley
12
Lanchester
A1(M)
A 691
DURHAM
Stanhope
A 689
Tow Law
A 688
Wolsingham
DURHAM
Crook
Bishop Auckland
A 177
HARTLEPOOL
B 6277
Middleton-in-Teesdale
West Auckland
11
Shildon
Sedgefield
CLEVELAND
Billingham
Redcar
B 6276
Staindrop
A 688
A 68
STOCKTON
MIDDLESBROUGH
Barnard Castle
A 67
A 66
Thornaby

MAP 1

CORNWALL

1 ST JUST Fore Street   Star
(St J 788767)
St Austell. Quaint old beamed town pub. Parking in nearby square. B & B. Substantial snacks. Yard with tables. Family/children's room opposite main bar with TV. Traditional beer.
On B3306 coast road in town centre.

2 ZENNOR   Tinner's Arms (St Ives 6927)
Free House. Old church house. Roadside parking. Snacks, garden and patio. Children allowed in lounge bar (when hatch is closed). Traditional beer.
Just off B3306 coast road in village 3m W of St Ives.

3 LAMORNA   Lamorna (Mousehole 566)
Devenish. 17th C stone; old 'kiddiwink'. Snacks available. Outside chairs and tables. End bar room used for children/family room. Traditional ale.
S off B3315, 1m.

4 HALSETOWN   Halsetown Inn
(St Ives 5583)
Devenish. Stone built pub with Cornish range in the room set aside for families. B & B. Lunches and evening meals. Small garden, back verandah also used for children. Traditional beer.
On B3311 in village centre.

5 LELANT   Badger (Hayle 752181)
St Austell. Private house converted. B & B. Bar meals day and evening. Garden and patio off which is a 'cubs' bar with soft drinks and games. Traditional beer.
On St Ives Road A3074 off A30.

6 CROWLAS   Star (Cockwells 375)
Courage. 19th C main road pub. B & B. Bar meals, garden. Family room and pool room off main entrance.
On A30 between Penzance and Hayle.

7 ST ERTH   Star (Hayle 752068)
Devenish. Small typical village pub, modernised. B & B. Meals & snacks. Garden. Children's room off main bar. Traditional beer.
On B3302, 2m S of Hayle.

8 GOLDSITHNEY   Crown
(Marazion 710494)
St Austell. Picturesque village pub. Roadside parking. B & B. Bar meals morning and evening. Family/children's room off main entrance. Traditional beer.
In village centre ½m N off A394.

9 ROSUDGEON   Falmouth Packet.
(Germoe 2240)
St Austell. Main road pub near Prussia Cove. Bar meals, limited in winter. Garden and picnic area. Children's room (old lounge bar) with soft drinks and sweets. Traditional beer.
On A394.

10 HAYLE (Loggans Mill)   Penmare
** (H 752031)
Bass. Converted private house. Bar meals. Children well catered for with paddling pool, sandpits. Family room with soft-drinks bar, games and own toilets off this area.
On A30 near B3301.

11 PRAZE (St Erth)   Smugglers
* (Leedstown 280)
Free House. Country pub with smuggling associations. B & B. Restaurant, snacks. Outdoor and indoor facilities for children on enclosed verandah.
On B3302 Hayle/Helston road.

12 BREAGE   Queen's Arms
* (Helston 3485)
Devenish. Victorian pub with fine collection of Jubilee china, etc. B & B. Bar meals all times. Garden. Family room with TV, games and own soft drinks bar. Traditional beer.
N just off A394, in village by church, 2m W of Helston.

13 HELSTON Coinagehall Street
Blue Anchor (H 62821)
Free House. One of the country's original home-brew houses, still brewing. 16th C old world atmosphere. Restricted street parking. Limited snacks. Two family rooms with amusements. Traditional beer.
In town centre on A394.

14 GWITHIAN (nr Hayle)   Pendarve's Arms
(Hayle 753223)
Devenish. Victorian roadside pub. Bar meals. Garden. Stable converted for family room.
On B3301 at T-junction in village.

15 PORKELLIS   Star
(Constantine 40237)
Devenish. Old country pub off the beaten track. Bar snacks, limited in winter. Garden. Stable loft converted to children's room with amusements.
1½m W off A394 between Helston and Penryn.

MAP 1

16 RAME Halfway House
(Stithians 860222)
Devenish. Old main road pub. Restaurant open all year. Bar meals, children's meals. Children's/family room with games (own soft drinks bar open in high season) in converted garage. Traditional beer.
On A394 between Helston and Penryn.

17 HELFORD Shipwrights
(Manacean 235)
Devenish. Old waterside pub. Small car park but prohibited traffic in summer. Meals and snacks. Picturesque garden. Part covered patio for families in bad weather. Traditional beer.
3m E and then N off B3291 S of Gweek.

18 MAWNAN SMITH Red Lion
(MS 250026)
Devenish. 16th C thatched village pub. Snacks all times. Small patio. Children's room with games at back. Traditional ale.
S of Falmouth 2m off B3291.

19 FALMOUTH Bar Road Dock and Railway (F 314324)
Devenish. Victorian pub modernised. Substantial snacks. Tables and chairs outside. Large family room with games off hallway. Traditional beer.
At end of A39 by dock gate.

20 PERRANARWORTHAL Norway
(Devoran 862081)
Devenish. One time small quayside pub. B & B. Buffet and restaurant. Bar meals. Attractive garden. Unique all-weather family patio at back. Traditional beer.
On A39 S of Truro.

**21 PENPOL (nr Truro)
Punchbowl & Ladle** (Devoran 862237)
Devenish. Old thatched one-time Excise office. B & B. Restaurant, bar meals. Patio. Small children's room off lounge bar and daytime use of long bar when wet. Traditional beer.
Off A38, SW of Truro, on King Harry Ferry road.

22 TRURO Pydar Street City Inn (T 2623)
Courage. Old market pub with public car park nearby and restricted roadside parking. Lunches (except Sun). Substantial snacks all times. Garden. Small family room. Traditional ale.
In city centre on main road by cattle market.

23 TRURO High Town County Arms
(T 3972)
Devenish. Modern main-road pub. Buffet (not weekends) and lunches. Evening meals (not Sun). Small garden with large children's area, part under main building covered. Games, minerals bar.
On A390 near County Hall.

24 PORTREATH Basset Arms (P 842254)
Devenish. Small seaside pub. Bar meals. Tables and chairs outside. Children's room over bar store.
On B3301 overlooking sea.

25 PORTREATH The Square Portreath
(P 842259)
Devenish. Victorian seaside town pub. Bar meals summer. Lunches only winter. Tables and chairs on forecourt. Family room. Traditional beer. Caravan parking.
On B3301 Redruth side of village near beach.

**26 PERRANPORTH The Square
Tywarnhayle** (P 2215)
Devenish. Old mines house rebuilt. Car park with restricted street parking. Lunches. Snacks evenings. Patio with soft-drinks bar. Pool room and family room upstairs.
On B3255 near beach.

27 PERRANZABULOE White House
** (Perranporth 3306)
Free House. One-time school. Restaurant. Bar meals. Play area, swings, swimming pool (charged) and children's corner with amusements and own food and mineral bar.
On A3075 cross roads E of Perranporth.

28 WEST PENTIRE Crantock Bowgie
** (Crantock 363)
Free House. Isolated on the point overlooking the sea, an old farm house. B & B. Meals. Garden. Children's room off the bar. Traditional beer.
3m off A3075.

29 NEWQUAY Jolly Sailor (N 2838)
Devenish. Trendy, modern centre-of-town pub, next to public car park. Meals all times. Buffet lunch. Covered patio for families alongside main street.
On one-way system leading to Towan Head from centre.

30 NEWQUAY North Quay Hill Red Lion
(N 2195)
Devenish. An old coaching stop. Limited

MAP 1

parking, nearby paying parks. B & B. Meals. Beer garden. Patio (seasonal) at back, covered. Fine views over harbour. Traditional beer.
On one-way system near the quay.

31 LADOCK Falmouth Arms
(Grampound 882319)
St Austell. One-time coaching stop. B & B. Bar snacks, garden. Children's room with pool table. Traditional beer.
On A39 N of Truro on main Bodmin road.

32 FRADDON Blue Anchor (F 252)
St Austell. Old coaching stop. B & B. Bar meals. Hut in garden for high season, soft-drinks bar. Traditional beer.
On A30 in village centre.

33 ST COLUMB MAJOR New Inn
(StCM 880485)
Devenish. Old beamed small pub. Limited parking, restricted roadside. Substantial bar snacks. Courtyard. Children's room upstairs and use of pool room. Traditional ale.
Off A3059 Wadebridge end of town.

34 ST MAWGAN Falcon (StM 225)
Free House. Village pub of character. Meals. Garden with special children's soft-drinks bar.
Off B3276 in village centre.

35 PADSTOW Lanadwell Street
Golden Lion (P 532797)
Devenish. Quaint old seaside-town pub. Parking limited and restricted. Bar snacks. Patio at back. Children's room (family room in winter) off passageway.
At end of A389, ¼m from harbour.

36 POLGOOTH Polgooth (St Austell 4089)
St Austell. One-time farmhouse converted in small country village. B & B. Bar meals all times. Garden with farm animals. Games. Children's room with own bar in season. Traditional beer.
Off A390 S of St Austell.

37 PAR Royal (P 4126)
Devenish. Old railway hotel. B & B. Snacks, garden. Small family room with TV off main bar. Traditional beer.
On A308 Lostwithiel road out of Par.

38 LANREATH Punchbowl (L 218)
Free House. Famous old Cornish village pub off the beaten track. Accommodation. Restaurant. Bar meals. Garden. Accompanied children use the Kitchen bar,

off main entrance. Traditional beer.
Off B3359 NW of Looe.

39 DOBWALLS Highwayman (D 20363)
Courage. Victorian main-road pub. Lunches and dinners (limited on Mon and Tues eve). Terrace. Children's/family room alongside main bar off car park.
On A38 2m W of Liskeard.

40 WIDEMOUTH BAY Widemouth Manor
WB 263269)
Free House. One-time manor house. B & B. Meals. Garden and views. Family/children's room through main bar off garden.
1m W off A39.

41 LOWER METHERELL Carpenter's Arms
(St Dominick 50242)
Free House. Quaint, hard-to-find village pub. Accommodation. Bar meals. Garden, patio. Children's room. Traditional beer.
1½m off B3254 S of Launceston.

42 MOUNT EDGCUMBE (Cremyll)
* **Edgcumbe Arms** (Plymouth 82224)
Courage. Old ferry house on waterside. Large free parking area. Snacks all times. Outside seating. Large family room with pool table. Traditional beer.
At end of B3241.

DEVON (see also Map 2)

43 HARTLAND King's Arms (H 222)
Free House. Old smuggling pub. Small children's room opposite main bar. Traditional beer.
On B3248 2½m W of A39 in village centre.

44 MORTEHOE Chichester Arms
(Woolacombe 411)
Watneys. Character pub with smuggling associations. Bar meals, patio. Garage converted for children's room. Traditional beer.
½m N of Woolacombe on coast road.

45 COMBE MARTIN Seaside Hill Dolphin
(CM 3424)
Free House. Overlooking the cove. Limited parking. Buffet lunches. Summer evening snacks. Back patio, part-covered, with children's games and a parrot. Traditional ale.
On A399 Ilfracombe end of town.

MAP 1

46 WEST DOWN (nr Ilfracombe)
* **Fox Hunter** (Ilfracombe 63757)
Free House. Quaint old coaching house full of nicknacks and an old coach. Restaurant open at all times. Bar meals and substantial snacks. Garden. Old public bar used as children's room.
On A361 S of Ilfracombe.

47 BLACKMOOR GATE Old Station (Parracombe 274)
Free House. Enlarged, converted railway station. Restaurant, bar meals, garden. Children's room in front porch.
On A39 at A399 turn off.

48 BRAUNTON Agriculture (B 812169)
Bass. Unusual country-town pub. Snacks. Small porch and patio. Use of skittle alley for children if with parents.
On A361 north end of town.

49 BRATTON FLEMING White Hart (Brayford 344)
Free House. Exmoor country pub. Bar snacks. Garden. Children's room by main entrance with games. Traditional ale.
1m off A3226 in village.

50 BARNSTAPLE The Square Mogfords Golden Lion (B 2715)
Devenish. Quaint old town pub with slab stone floors. Restricted parking. Snacks mornings. Games room off passage for children's use, and seats in passage. Traditional beer.
On A39 by bridge roundabout in town centre.

51 BARNSTAPLE Exeter (B 71052)
Watneys. Quaint old carriers' pub. Lunches (except Sun). Snacks other times. Tables in yard. Children can use skittle alley or small front room.
Off A39 on road parallel with Taunton road.

52 BIDEFORD Silver Street Portobello (B 3257)
Courage. Market pub with limited parking in Pannier Market. Bar snacks. Small back barn attic converted as a games room for accompanied children. Traditional beer.
On one-way system on the hill.

53 BEAFORD Globe (B 261)
Free House. Quaint old village pub, one-time coaching change. B & B. Substantial bar meals. Garden. Small children's room off the 'bar at the back'.

Traditional beer.
On B3220 in village centre.

54 MEETH Winged Bull (Hatherleigh 235)
Free House. Old 16th C church house. Bar meals, garden. Side room available for accompanied children. Traditional beer.
On A386 Okehampton/Bideford road.

55 WINKLEIGH High Street Seven Stars (W 344)
Free House. Small town pub with yard. Unrestricted parking. Bar snacks. garden. Barn with amusements for children when wet. Traditional beer.
W ¼m off B3220 in village.

56 LAPFORD Old Malt Scoop (L 330)
Free House. Quaint old village pub. B & B. Restaurant evenings, lunches. Garden. Fishing rights. Porch where children can sit (with notice, a room is available). Traditional beer.
1m E of A377 in village centre.

57 SAMPFORD COURTENAY New Inn
* (N Tawton 247)
Heavitree. 16th C roadside pub. Buffet including seafoods. Garden. Children's room off the eating area. Traditional ale.
On A3072 holiday route to N Cornwall.

58 BEACON CROSS (Sampford Courtenay) Countryman (N Tawton 206)
Free House. Modern pub specialising in eating. Restaurant. Garden. Small children's room off main bar with door to garden.
On B3215 4m E of Okehampton.

59 YEOFORD Mare & Foal (Copplestone 348)
Free House. Once the railway hotel, now typical village pub. B & B. Meals available. Garden. Large area for children off the lounge bar, part of which is the skittle alley. Traditional beer.
3m W off A377, 1m N of Crediton.

60 LEWDOWN Blue Lion (L 235)
Free House. Old main-road coaching change. B & B. Substantial bar snacks lunchtime and w/e evenings. Garden. Children's snug off main bar and long verandah in entrance. Traditional beer.
On A30 between Launceston and Okehampton.

61 LYDFORD Castle (L 242)
Free House. 16th C picturesque village

MAP 1

pub. Accommodation. Buffet lunches, evening meals. Garden. Quaint little children's room with settles. Traditional ale.
1m W off A386 in village centre next to castle.

62 BRENTOR (W Dartmoor) Brentor
(Mary Tavy 240)
Whitbread. Small isolated Dartmoor pub near the church. Snacks. Garden, views. Covered entrance verandah for children's room.
2m W off A386 in Mary Tavy.

63 PRINCETOWN Devil's Elbow (P 232)
Courage. Name refers to the sharp bend in the disused railway. Meals mornings and evenings. Verandah porch to back bar used as a children's room in wet weather. Traditional beer.
On B3212 in village centre.

64 HEXWORTHY (Princetown) Forest
* (Poundsgate 211)
Free House. In the heart of Dartmoor. B & B. Restaurant, bar meals and snacks. Facilities for children in the lounge or covered ways between outhouses.
1m off B3357.

65 SCORRITON Tradesman's Arms
(Poundsgate 206)
Free House. Small country pub on outskirts of Dartmoor. B & B. Substantial bar meals. Picturesque garden. Suntrap children's room. Traditional ale.
Off B3357 1m, in village.

66 HOLNE Church House
(Poundsgate 208)
Free House. 14th C in parts. High up on the moor. B & B. Substantial bar meals. Dining room used as family room. Traditional ale and own mead.
Off A38 2½m NW of Buckfast.

67 BUCKFASTLEIGH Globe (B 2223)
Whitbread. Victorian country town pub. Bar meals, patio, children's room off the main bar and car park. Traditional beer.
W off A38 in town centre.

68 STAVERTON (nr Totnes) Sea Trout
(Staverton 274)
Free House. Part was the old church house, now a large village pub. B & B. Restaurant evenings and Sunday lunch. Bar meals. Garden. Children's room off car park entrance.
Off A384 in village.

69 STARCROSS (Cockwood) Ship
(S 373)
Courage. Converted private house with rambling bars. Hot and cold buffet. Garden with streamside tables. Children's room partitioned off in the food area.
Just off A379 coast road, by inlet.

70 DAWLISH WARREN Mount Pleasant
** Road Mount Pleasant
(Dawlish 863151)
Heavitree. A rebuilt pub with smugglers' stories and a wonderful view. Buffet bar. Substantial bar meals. Garden. Children's room leading to garden. Games room alongside main bar.
On the A379 at top of hill.

71 DAWLISH Brunswick Place Brunswick
Heavitree. A small town pub by the stream with ducks and swans. Limited parking. Snacks in bar. Seasonal play room in skittle alley or seats in covered passage all the year.
Just off A379 on the town's one-way system from the sea front.

72 SHALDON Fore Street Clifford Arms
(S 2311)
Bass. Small village pub. Roadside parking. Bar meals and snacks all times. Garden with a children's room with games, also pool room in pub. Traditional beer.
Just off A379 in village.

73 MAIDENCOMBE (nr Torquay)
Old Thatch (Torquay 39155)
Free House. A pretty thatched cottage with modern pub alongside. Limited parking. Light meals in bar. Cream teas. Garden. Children's play room alongside. (Seasonal Licence.)
E ¼m off A379 north of Torquay, ¼m from sea.

74 KINGSKERSWELL Manor Road
Hare & Hounds (K 3119)
Heavitree. Modern roadside pub. Substantial bar meals. Garden. Children's room with games and own sweets/soft-drinks bar.
On A380 3m out of Torquay.

75 MARLDON Church House
(Paignton 558279)
Whitbreads. Said to be 13th C, old stone building with open fireplaces. Adequate bar snacks. Large garden. Children's room as part of skittle alley over old stabling.
1m W of A3022 Torbay loop road.

MAP 1

76 ST BUDEAUX (Plymouth)
Saltash Passage Ferry House
(Plymouth 361659)
Courage. Old waterside pub. Lunches mid-week, snacks weekends and evenings. Children's room off the lounge with glass partition. Traditional beer.
Just below toll bridge on A38.

77 SOUTH BRENT Woodpecker (SB 2125)
Free House. A Victorian pub. Restaurant (weekends). Bar meals daily. Garden. Restaurant used as children's room daily and evenings (except Fri and Sat).
On A385 at junction with A38.

78 RINGMORE Journey's End
(Bigbury-on-Sea 205)
Free House. An old pub in a tiny village 15 mins walk to the sea. Extensive bar meals. Evening restaurant (except Sun). Garden. Children's room off the main bar. Traditional beer.
Off B3392 Bigbury road.

79 MODBURY Exeter (M 239)
Watneys. 16th C half-timbered pub famed for its food. B & B. Restaurant evenings (except Sun). Bar meals other times. Garden. Children allowed in the lounge under supervision. Traditional ale.
On A379 Plymouth/Kingsbridge road in village centre.

80 ST ANN'S CHAPEL Pickwick
(Bigbury-on-Sea 241)
Free House. 13th C chapel alongside. B & B. Substantial bar meals. Large garden. Chapel used as children's room complete with games. Traditional beer.
On B3392 Bigbury road.

81 BANTHAM Sloop (Thurlestone 489)
Free House. Old fishermen's and holiday pub. B & B. Hot and cold meals night and day. Beer garden. Children's room in buffet bar until 8pm (unless eating). Traditional ale.
3m off A379 roundabout to W.

82 SALCOMBE Fore Street
Burners Victoria (S 2604)
Free House. Small old seaside pub. Very limited parking nearby. Snacks available. Garden at back. Children's room in outhouse off the garden.
At end of A381 overlooking sea.

83 FROGMORE Globe (F 351)
Free House. Victorian village pub with unrestricted street parking. B & B. Res-

taurant (every day in summer). Bar meals. Family room next to restaurant. Traditional beer.
On A379 halfway between Torcross and Kingsbridge.

84 BEESANDS Cricket Inn (Torcross 215)
** Heavitree. Seafront fishermen's cottages converted. No parking problems. Substantial snacks all times. Patio and large children's room with games. Softdrinks bar high season.
2½m S off A379 in Stokenham. Narrow Devon lanes.

85 SLAPTON Tower (Torcross 216)
Free House. Old stone pub up a dead-end lane. Cordon bleu restaurant. Bar meals and snacks. Children's/family room at opposite end of building to snack bar. Traditional beer.
1½m off A379 Dartmouth/Torcross road.

86 HARBERTONFORD Maltsters Arms
(H 258)
Heavitree. A quaint old roadside pub. Hot pasties. Family room off the passageway.
On A381 4m S of Totnes.

87 BRIXHAM Fore Street Globe (B 2154)
Courage. Small town pub (in a daytime pedestrian precinct in summer.) B & B. Restaurant open in summer. Bar meals and snacks. Family room off coaching entrance. Traditional ale.
In one-way street from sea front (closed in summer).

88 CHURSTON FERRERS
Weary Ploughman (Torbay 2280)
Courage. Old railway hotel modernised. Bar meals and platter bar. Garden. Platter bar available for children under adult supervision only.
On A3022.

89 STOKE GABRIEL Victoria & Albert
(SG 216)
Whitbread. Rambling Victorian pub. Bar meals and snacks. Garden. Family room off the car park.
2m W off A3022.

EXMOOR

90 PORLOCK Ship (P 862507)
Free House. Famous old character pub. B & B and evening meal. Substantial bar

MAP 1

snacks. Garden at back and family room off main bar. Traditional beer.
On A39 at bottom of notorious Porlock Hill.

91 WHEDDON CROSS   Rest and be ** Thankful (Timberscombe 222)

Free House. Coaching house high up on Exmoor. Bar snacks (except Sun eve). Patio, garden, swings, roundabouts and extensive family room with games and soft-drinks bar. Traditional beer.
At crossroads B3224 and A396 on Exmoor.

MAP 1
Other pubs to try
CORNWALL

BOLVENTOR   Jamaica Inn   Shop, amusements, views and amenities
BUDE   Crooklets   Patio, children's facilities
BUDE   Falcon   Lawns and canalside
CADGWITH   Cadgwith   Garden, play area
CALLINGTON   Old Clink   Pooh Corner
CARGREEN   Spaniards   Children's facilities and riverside
CRANTOCK   Sea Gull   Garden and children's facilities with amusements
DOWNDERRY (nr Torpoint)   Sea View Inn Sea views and garden
FALMOUTH (Prislow Lane)   Boslowick   Children's games room
GOLANT (Fowey)   Fisherman's Arms   Views of river, children's facilities
GORRAN HAVEN   Llanwnroc   Lawns and views
HOLYWELL (Crantock, nr Newquay)   Treguth Inn   Terraced gardens near beach
LANIVET   Lanivet   Garden and play area
LAUNCESTON   Bell   Children's facilities and games room
MORWENSTOW   Bush   Wide-open spaces on commonland
MOUNT HAWKE   Mount Hawke   Grounds and animals
MULLION   Old Inn   Garden, children's facilities
NEWQUAY   Fort   Garden and children's facilities
PADSTOW   Harbour Inn   Children's facilities, patio, harbourside
PENSILVA   Victoria Inn   Animals and birds in garden
PENZANCE   London Inn   Children's garden
PHILLACK   New Inn   Playground
POLKERRIS   Rashleigh   Patio overlooking sea
POLPERRO   Three Pilchards   Quayside
POLZEATH   Polzeath   Children's facilities
PORT GAVERNE   Port Gaverne   Garden and sea views
PORTHLEVEN   Ship   Harbourside and sea views
RESTRONGUET   Pandora Inn   Waterside with moorings
ST MERRYN   Falmouth Arms   Children's facilities and garden
SALTASH   Bridge Inn   Views of Tamar, patio
SENNEN COVE   Old Success   Sea front, garden/patio
SENNEN COVE   Old Success   Sea Front, garden/patio
STITHIANS   Stithians   Own grounds
TRESCO (Scilly Isles)   New Inn   Garden and children's facilities
WATERGATE BAY   Chequers   Patio and children's facilities

DEVON (see also Map 2)

APPLEDORE   Beaver   Waterside patio
BICKINGTON   (Dartmoor) Halfway   Patio, play area
BRIXHAM   Blue Anchor   Children's facilities
CHALLACOMBE   Blue Venus   Play area
CLOVELLY   Red Lion   Waterside
CROYDE   Carpenter's Arms   Play area
DAWLISH   Railway   Children's amenities
DODDISCOMBSLEIGH   Nobody Inn   Play area
EAST PRAWLE   Pig's Nose   Play area
EXETER   Port Royal   Riverside, children's amenities

MAP 1

EXETER **Welcome** Quayside
HACKNEY (Kingskerswell) **Passage House** Waterside
HOLCOMBE **Smugglers** Play area
HOPE COVE **Hope & Anchor** Seaside, patio
IDDESLEIGH **Duke of York** Play area
LYNTON **Ship** Overlooking sea
NEWTON ABBOT **Pen** Children's amenities
NEWTON ABBOT **Ship** Play area with amenities in summer
NEWTON FERRERS **Dolphin** Play area, children's facilities
NEWTON ST CYRES **Crown & Sceptre** Swings and play garden
NORTH BOVEY **Ring o' Bells** Play area
PARRACOMBE **Hunter's Lodge** Garden, play area and birds
PLYMPTON **Lyneham Inn** Swings, slides, garden
POSTBRIDGE **Warren House** Shop and play area
SOUTH ZEAL **Rising Sun** Children's amenities
STRETE **King's Arms** Views and play area
THELBRIDGE **Thelbridge Arms** Play area
THORVERTON **Dolphin** Lawns and play area
TUCKENHAY **Waterman's Arms** Waterside
WELCOMBE **Old Smithy** Play area and children's facilities
WITHERIDGE **Angel** Children's facilities
WRAFTON **Williams Arms** Play area
YARD DOWN (North Molton) **Poltimore Arms** Children's facilities and Exmoor
YELVERTON **Foxhunter** Garden, play area

EXMOOR

DULVERTON **Caernarvon Arms** Play area and amenities
EXEBRIDGE **Anchor** Riverside garden
LUXBOROUGH **White Hart** Play area
PORLOCK WEIR **Ship** Overlooking quay
SANDYWAY **Sportsman** Moors
SIMONSBATH **Crown** Play area

MAP 2

EAST DEVON (see also Map 1)

1 CULMSTOCK Ilminster Arms
(Craddock 40414)
Whitbread. Old coaching house. B & B,
bar snacks. Small garden. Children's/
family room at back. Traditional beer.
1m E off A38 on B3397, in village, 4m
from J27 M6.

2 CLYST HYDON Five Bells
* (Plymtree 288)
Free House. 17th C country pub. Isol-
ated. Buffet bar, bar meals. Garden with
aviary. Children's room off main bar.
Traditional beer.
E off A38 Hele Cross. 2½m of narrow
lanes.

3 WHIMPLE Country House
Free House. Large main-road coaching
house. Restaurant, cafeteria, bar
snacks, garden. Children's room alongside cafeteria.
On A30.

4 SOWTON Highwayman
(Topsham 3317)
Free House. Part old chapel, modernised,
enlarged. Bar meals. Garden and holiday
camp. Children's shop and playroom off
car park. Traditional beer.
On A3052. 3m E of J30 M5.

5 EXMOUTH Queen's (E 72091)
Whitbread. Typical Victorian town pub.
B & B. Bar snacks. Children's room off
main bar.
A377 in town centre, on road to beach.

6 SIDMOUTH Old Fore Street Old Ship
(S 2127)
Free House. Old beamed town pub
c1550. Restaurant (open summer). Bar
meals. Table and chairs in back yard.
Small children's room off main street.
Traditional beer.
In town centre on one-way street.

7 SIDFORD Blue Ball (Sidmouth 4062)
* Devenish. Old-fashioned main-road pub.
B & B. Substantial bar meals. Garden.
Barbecue Sat when fine. Large family
room (stable bar). Traditional beer.
On B3052.

**8 GITTISHAM COMMON Putts Corner
Hare & Hounds** (Honiton 2987)
Free House. Isolated country pub. Bar
snacks. Garden, aviary and pets' corner.
Children's barn at back with games.
Traditional beer.
On A375 crossroads with B3174 south
of Honiton.

9 COLYTON King Street The Bear
* (C 52256)
Free House. An old pub in an old country
village. Small garden with skittle alley as
children's room with games, in season.
Snacks. Traditional ale.
In village centre on B3161.

**10 COLYTON Market Place
Colcombe Castle** (C 52257)
Free House. In centre of village. B & B,
meals. Family room with games and
children's room. Traditional ale.
In village centre in square on B3161.

11 COLYFORD (Seaton) White Hart
(Colyton 52358)
Bass. Main-road pub. Bar meals. Tram
stop. Large children's room at back with
games (in use summer only).
On A3052 in small village N of Seaton.

12 UPLYME New Inn (Lyme Regis 3210)
Palmers. Small quaint village pub. Bar
meals. Patio. Small children's room off
bar. Traditional ale.
On A3070 in village. 1½m NW of Lyme
Regis.

13 AXMINSTER Millwey (A 32774)
Palmers. Modern estate pub. Bar meals,
patio and play area. Children's room
through public bar in skittle alley. Traditional beer.
On A358 1m on Chard road.

SOMERSET

14 CARHAMPTON Butcher's Arms
(Dunster 333)
Watneys, 17th C pub with church
associations. B & B. Bar meals. Garden.
Family room off lounge bar.
On A39 in village centre.

15 BLUE ANCHOR Blue Anchor
(Washford 239)
Bass. Rebuilt old smugglers' haunt.
Meals, buffet. Garden and children's
amusement bar off the car park.
Off A39 overlooking bay.

16 WATCHET West Somerset (W 31483)
Watneys. Old railway (from mines) pub
near docks. B & B, bar meals. Courtyard
and skittle alley for family room (except

MAP 2

Sun eve).
N 1m off A39 in village centre.

17 WASHFORD   Washford (W 256)
Watneys. Once railway hotel, now Victorian roadside pub. B & B. Restaurant, bar meals. Garden. Children's/family room with games.
On A39.

18 LANGLEY MARSH   Three Horseshoes
(Wiveliscombe 33763)
Free House. Typical village pub on Quantock foothills. B & B, substantial snacks. Garden. Small children's room. Traditional beer.
W off B3188 1m N of Wiveliscombe.

**19 BRIDGWATER Wembdon Road
Quantock Gateway** (B 3593)
Whitbread. One-time brewery on Minehead road. B & B, lunches, snacks evenings. Garden with swings and frame. Conservatory as family room. Traditional beer.
On A39 road out of Bridgwater to Minehead.

20 BURNHAM-ON-SEA Pier Street   Pier
(B 783161)
Free House. Victorian pub overlooking bay. Public car park opposite. B & B. Restaurant (closed Sun eve.) Bar meals. Children's room with TV and books off main bar. Traditional beer.
3m W of J22 M5 near front.

**21 BURNHAM-ON-SEA Abbingdon St
Somerset & Dorset** (B 783150)
Whitbread. Typical Victorian seaside pub. Restricted parking. Snacks. Children's room off passage to lounge.
3m W off J22 M5 on main street.

22 WEST HUNTSPILL   Crossways
(Burnham 783756)
Free House. Coaching change house. Bar meals. Garden with children's/family room off it. Traditional beer.
On A38 2½m S of J22 M5.

**23 BLACKFORD (nr Wedmore)
Sexey's Arms** (Wedmore 712487)
Courage. Picturesque old country pub of character. Restaurant (not Mon, Tues, Wed eve). Bar meals. Garden. Use of skittle alley as family room, or porch for children. Traditional beer.
On B3139, 4m W of Wedmore.

24 KEINTON MANDEVILLE   Quarry

(Charlton Mackrell 367)
Free House. One-time quarry owner's house, a main road pub in quiet village. B & B, bar snacks. Garden. Family room off main bar. Traditional beer.
On B3153 1m W of A37.

25 EAST PENNARD   Traveller's Rest
(Datchet 338)
Courage. One-time coaching stop, main-road pub. Restaurant, home-cooked meals. Garden with swings and frame. Skittle alley with children's amusements. Traditional ale.
On A37 Fosse Way, 5m S of Shepton Mallet.

26 LOVINGTON   Pilgrim's Rest
(Wheathill 310)
Free House. 16th C old pilgrims' rest house on main road. B & B, bar meals. Garden with slides. Use of skittle alley as family room. Traditional beer.
On B3153 2m W of Castle Cary.

27 WINCANTON   Hunters Lodge
(Bourton 439)
Free House. One-time royal hunting lodge. Buffet, bar meals. Patio. Use of skittle alley for children. Traditional beer.
On A303 2m E of Wincanton.

28 EMBOROUGH   Old Down
(Stratton-on-the-Fosse 232398)
Free House. Famous old coaching house on main road. Accommodation, bar meals. Swimming pool for residents. Several children's rooms with games. Traditional ale.
Just off A39, 4m N of Shepton Mallet.

29 OLDFORD (nr Frome)   Ship
(Frome 2043)
Watneys. Victorian main-road pub on Bath road. Bar meals. Garden. Large covered yard at the back, off the garden. Traditional beer.
On A361, 2m N of Frome.

30 WOOLVERTON   Red Lion
(Beckington 350)
Wadworth. Character pub near the tropical bird sanctuary. Bar meals (French cuisine winter). Garden. Little bay room for families off the main bar. Traditional beer.
On A36 Frome/Bath road.

31 NORTON ST PHILIP   George
(Faulkland 224)
Wadworth. One of England's oldest and

MAP 2

most historic houses. Roadside parking. Restaurant and bar meals. Courtyard patio and large family room in ancient lounge at end of corridor. Traditional beer.
On A3110 in village centre.

32 FARLEIGH HUNGERFORD
Hungerford Arms (Trowbridge 2411)
Watneys. Old tything house of the estate. Dining room (closed Sun eve). Buffet. Patio garden with views. Family room off garden and lounge bar. Traditional beer.
1½m E on A36.

AVON

33 UPHILL (nr Weston) Ship
(Weston-super-Mare 21470)
Whitbread. Victorian village local, ¼m from beach. Roadside parking. Lunches (not Sun). Snacks evenings. Garden, children's room off garden yard or main bar.
1m S of Weston-s-Mare off A370.

34 WESTON-SUPER-MARE Alexandra
Parade Foresters (WsM 21280)
Courage. Victorian main-road pub. Restricted parking. Meals and buffet. Yard and shed converted for children's use. Traditional beer.
In town centre.

35 WESTON-SUPER-MARE High Street
London (WsM 20208)
Bass. Victorian town-centre pub. No parking. Public park nearby. Substantial snacks in bar (children's portions). Children's/family room with amusements.
In town centre.

36 SAND BAY Long John Silver
(WsM 23367)
Wadworths. Right on sea front with miles of sands. Meals (limited in winter). Garden in front. Large children's room with games. Traditional beer.
On coast 1m N of Weston-super-Mare via toll road.

37 BANWELL Ship (B 822522)
* Courage. Old hanging judge's headquarters after Monmouth rebellion, his court room now the family room. Snacks. Traditional beer.
On A371 at junction with A368 3m E of Weston-super-Mare.

38 CONGRESBURY Plough
(Yatton 832475)
Courage. Character pub on Taunton road. Snacks, garden in front and family room with TV and pin tables off main bar.
Off A370 in village centre.

39 CLEEVE Lord Nelson (Yatton 832170)
Courage. Stately Victorian pub. Snacks. Play area. Family room off main entrance between both bars. Traditional beer.
On A370 2m N of Congresbury.

40 CLAPTON-IN-GORDANO Black Horse
(Portishead 842105)
Courage. Quaint 17th C pub beneath the motorway. Snacks. Patio. Family room off main entrance in rambling bar.
Off B3124 Portishead/Clevedon Road, 4m from J19 M5.

41 BARROW GURNEY Prince's Motto
(BG 83130)
Free House. Old stone village pub. Bar meals (except Sun). Garden. Vinery used as family room (cold in winter). Traditional beer.
Just off A38 W into village.

42 CHEW MAGNA Pony & Trap
(CM 2627)
Free House. Old farm cottages with views. Bar meals. Garden with family room off it (only until 8pm).
S off B3130 1m out of village.

43 WEST HARPTREE Wells Way
(WH 382)
Free House. Isolated. Restaurant, bar meals. Gardens with swings and chute. Family room off car park. Traditional beer.
1m S of West Harptree in the Mendip Hills.

44 LITTON King's Arms
* (Chewton Mendip 301)
Free House. Associated with Charles II's escape in the Civil War. Picturesque garden with swings and slides. Family room off main bar and at back. Traditional ale.
1m W off B3114 off A39.

45 PENSFORD High Street George &
Dragon (Compton Dando 516)
Free House. One-time coaching house. B & B, bar meals, garden and family room off yard at the back. Traditional ale.
E off A37 in village, signed Compton Dando.

MAP 2

46 CLUTTON HILL   Hunter's Rest
(Temple Cloud 52303)
Free House. Isolated, fine views. Bar
meals, buffet. Garden with swings and
slides. Children's room in garden with
seasonal soft-drinks bar. Traditional ale.
E off A39 along narrow lane.

47 CAMERTON   Jolly Collier
(Timsbury 70491)
Free House. Enormous miner in forecourt
of modernized mining pub. Bar meals.
Garden, play area. Children's room off
main bar.
E off A367 in village on side road.

48 HINTON   Bull (Abson 2332)
Wadworth. Cotswold stone farm house.
Substantial bar meals. Garden and
adventure play area. Converted stabling
used as family room with games. Traditional beer.
1½m W off A46 ½m from J18 M4.

49 TORMARTON   Compass
(Badminton 242)
Free House. Old stone-built pub of char-
acter. B & B, hot and cold buffet. Gar-
den. Families, lunchtime only, have use
of orangery, through buffet eating area.
Traditional beer.
Just off motorway J18 N ½m.

50 WESTERLEIGH   Ye Olde Inn
(Chipping Sodbury 312344)
Courage. Old church house in village
centre. Dining room. Bar meals.
Children's menu all times. Garden. 2
children's/family rooms at end of pas-
sage and in old stable, with games.
Traditional beer.
E off A432 in village. 3m from J19 M4.

51 AUST   Boar's Head (Pilning 2278)
Courage. Small village pub just off
motorway. Bar snacks (except Sun
lunch). Garden. Family room with pool
table. Traditional ale. Camping site.
½m S of J21 M4.

52 THORNBURY   Royal George (T 412149)
Courage. 17th C coach house in town
centre. Garden with swings. Light
lunches and snacks. Family room off
main bar and meeting room used. Traditional beer.
On A38 3m S of J14 M5.

GLOUCESTERSHIRE (see also Map 5)

53 SHARPNESS   Pier View (S 255)
Whitbread. Typical Victorian pub over-
looking Severn. B & B. Snacks (meals by
arrangement). Garden with swings.
Families use pool room off passage.
At end of B4066 W off A38.

54 TETBURY   Crown (T 52469)
Whitbread. 17th C coaching house. Free
parking. B & B. Bar lunches and evening
meals. Small family room at back of
public bar, with TV and pool. Traditional
beer.
In town centre, off Market Place.

55 KEMBLE Tetbury Road   Thames Head
(K 259)
Free House. Typical country pub near the
river's source. Bar lunches and evening
meals. Garden. Family room off main
passage to the bars. Traditional ale.
On A438 Fosse Way.

56 AMPNEY CRUCIS   Crown (Poulton 403)
Free House. Old Chiltern stone cottages
converted. Restaurant, evenings (not
Wed). Bar meals all times. River bank.
Family room for over fives off bar on way
to restaurant. Traditional beer.
On A417 Fosse Way.

57 SOUTHROP   Swan (S 205)
Courage. Once the village morgue. Chiltern stone. Restaurant, bar lunches and
evening meals. Small garden with
swings. Family room off lounge bar.
On byroad 3m NW of Lechlade.

OXFORDSHIRE (see also Maps 3 & 5)

58 NEWBRIDGE (nr Witney)   Rose Revived
(Standlake 221)
Moreland. 16th C pub of character on
Thames. B & B. Restaurant. Bar meals.
Patio. Garden. Family room overlooking
river and off main bar. Traditional beer.
Just off A415 4m S of Witney.

59 FYFIELD Old Main Road   White Hart
(Frilford Heath 390585)
Free House. 15th C chantry house of
character. Restaurant. Bar meals. Garden. 'Minstrels' Gallery' as family room
up to 8pm. Traditional beer.
Off A420 Swindon/Oxford.

BERKSHIRE (see also Map 3)

60 EAST   ILSLEY   High   Street   Crown &

MAP 2

Horns (El 205)
Free House. 18th C coaching house of character. Bar meals (except Sun lunch). Patio. Children's/family room off main bar with TV. Traditional beer.
Just off A34 in village centre.

61 HUNGERFORD Charnham Street   Lamb (H 2782)
Courage. One-time minor coaching stage. Bar snacks. Garden, frame and tame goat. Children's room in garden. Traditional beer.
On A4 on E side of town.

WILTSHIRE

63 ASHTON KEYNES Back Street, nr Cricklade   Plough (AK 265)
Whitbread. Small farm cottages converted. Hard to find. Bar meals except Tues, when light snacks. Garden with swings. Family room off car park.
N off B4040, 2m E of Cricklade.

64 BROKENBOROUGH (nr Malmesbury)
** **Red Bull** (Malmesbury 2108)
Free House. Country pub. Snacks. Gardens. Family room in stabling with amusements, and children's bar open summer weekends.
On B4040 1½m W of Malmesbury.

65 WOOTTON BASSETT High Street Carriers (WB 2327)
Arkells. Small old town pub. B & B. Lunches Mon to Fri. Patio garden. Family room off lounge bar. Traditional ale.
3m off A420 from J16 M4 in town centre.

66 SUTTON BENGER   Vintage (Seafry 770240)
Wadworths. One-time brewery converted. B & B, bar meals, buffet, garden. Dining room used as children's room. Traditional beer.
SE 3m off J17 M4 to A420 in village.

67 CASTLE COMBE   White Hart
* (CC 782295)
Free House. In one of England's prettiest and oldest villages. Parking very restricted. Buffet all the year (hot choice in winter). Garden, children's patio and family room. Traditional beer.
W off B4039 in village centre.

68 BIDDESTONE (Chippenham)
White Horse (Corsham 713305)
Courage. 16th C monks' hospice on village green. Bar snacks. Village green and children's room.
N off A4 1½m W of Chippenham.

69 CORSHAM   Cross Keys (C 712323)
Watneys. Main-road old stone-built pub. Meals at lunchtime. Garden. Lounge bar, really a family room off the main bar. Traditional ale.
On A4 in town centre.

70 BOX   Northey Arms (B 2333)
Wadworths. Stone-built (1934) main-road pub. Restaurant. Buffet. Garden. Small vestibule used for children on wet days. Traditional beer.
On A4 W of village.

71 LIMPLEY STOKE Woods Hill   Hop Pole (LS 3134)
Courage. Quaint picturesque small village pub. Substantial bar snacks. Garden. Family room off lounge bar. Traditional ale.
Off A36 into village centre.

72 BRADFORD-ON-AVON (Woolley) George (BoA 3515)
Watneys. Old farmhouse off the beaten track. Snacks all times. Garden and small family room with pool table off main entrance.
Just off B3019, N side of town.

73 LOCKERIDGE (nr Marlborough) Who'd ha' Tho't It (L 255)
Wadworths. Old bakery converted, typical village pub. Substantial bar snacks. Small family room off main entrance. Large garden. Traditional beer.
2m SW of Marlborough. S off A4.

74 MARLBOROUGH St Martin's Street Queen's Head (M 52855)
Whitbread. In the back streets on Ramsbury Road. Snacks. Small family room off main passage. Traditional beer.
In town centre off A345.

75 RAMSBURY The Square   Bell (R 230)
Free House. quaint 16th C village pub. Restaurant (closed Sun eve and Mon all day). Bar meals lunchtime. Small family room with Spy prints and antique furniture. Traditional beer.
Off A419 3½m W of Hungerford in village square.

76 DEVIZES Hare & Hounds Street Hare & Hounds (D 3231)

MAP 2

Wadworths. Old 17th C back street pub off green. Snacks. Patio yard and family room off passage. Traditional beer. In the back streets off A302.

77 WEST LAVINGTON Churchill
(WL 2287)
Bass. Old pub named after the estate owners. Restaurant (not Mon eve). Bar meals. Garden with swings. Children's rooms with amusements off car park. Coaches welcome. Traditional beer. On A360 in village.

78 WOODBOROUGH Honey Street
* (nr Pewsey) Barge (W 238)
Courage. Old canal bargees' pub with boat trips in summer. B & B. Restaurant, bar meals, Canalside garden. Barn converted as family room. Traditional beer. Well worth finding. Through timber yard, 2½m on by-road W of Pewsey.

79 PEWSEY Marlborough Road
French Horn (P 2443)
Wadworths. Old canal workers' house, then tied cottages. Bar meals day and evening. Gardens and small family room off main bar. Traditional beer. N of town on A345.

80 MILTON LILBOURNE Three Horseshoes
* * (Pewsey 2323)
Free House. Old Frome brewery, now pub. Restaurant, bar meals. Gardens with peacocks. Family hut with games. Caravan facilities. Traditional beer. 1m E of Pewsey on B3087.

81 CORSLEY White Hart (C 498)
* * Free House. Old coaching house near Longleat's lions. Restaurant (closed Sun eve and Mon). Lawns. Children's room with amusements by entrance. Traditional beer. On A362 Frome/Warminster road.

82 STOURHEAD Spread Eagle
(Bourton 587)
Free House. Home farm of Stourhead House built by Hoare the banker. B & B. Restaurant (evenings). Bar meals. Children's room in stabling. Traditional beer. N off A303 at Zeals in small hamlet.

83 ZEALS Bell & Crown (Bourton 227)
Watneys. One-time coaching change on main Exeter road. Cold buffet. Garden. Family room off lounge bar. On A303 in village centre.

84 DURRINGTON Stonehenge
(Durrington Walls 52423)
Whitbread. Large between-wars pub. Bar meals. Play area. Family room off main bar. On A345.

85 WILTON The Square Greyhound
(W 3600)
Watneys. An old coaching pub. Bar meals. Patio and garden. Family room off main bar. Traditional beer. In village square on A30.

DORSET

86 LYME REGIS Mill Green Angel
(LR 3267)
Palmers. Victorian pub in the back streets with a ghost. B & B. Snacks hot and cold. Garden. Small children's room off main bar (except Thurs eve). Traditional beer. N off A3052 at traffic lights.

87 LYME REGIS Coombe Street Ship
(LR 3681)
Palmers. Off the main road. Victorian pub with very restricted street parking. Snacks in season. Children's room off back bar with patio garden. N off A3052 at traffic lights.

89 SHAVE CROSS (Marshwood Vale)
Shave Cross (Broadwinsor 358)
Free House. A picturesque thatched isolated pub. Bar meals. Beamed bars, picturesque garden. Part of old skittle alley for children's use in summer (winter only at lunchtime). Closed Mon. Traditional beer. 2m E off B3165 Axminster/Broadwinsor road.

90 CHIDEOCK George (C 419)
Palmers. Old thatched main-road pub. B & B, bar meals, snacks. Garden. Family room off main entrance. Traditional beer. On A35 east end of village.

91 BRIDPORT South Street Ship
(B 24617)
Palmers. Small town pub with restricted parking. B & B. Snacks lunchtime. Garden. Family room off passage and use of skittle alley. Traditional beer. On B3157 in town centre.

92 SHIPTON (nr Bridport) Traveller's Rest
(B 23270)

MAP 2

Palmers. Old coaching stage. B & B. Restaurant. Bar meals. Garden. Children's barn at back. Traditional beer. Camping site.
On A35 3m E of Bridport.

93 SWYRE The Bull
** (Burton Bradstock 250)
Devenish. Old site of rebuilt pub. Bar meals. Gardens and large hay loft used as family room with amusements. Traditional beer.
On B3157 4m SE of Bridport.

94 ABBOTSBURY Ilchester Arms
(Abbotsbury 243)
Devenish. Quaint old stone house, once part of Ilchester Estate. B & B. Bar meals. Garden and large family room near entrance. Near swannery and tropical gardens. Traditional beer.
On B3157 coast road in village centre.

95 CATTISTOCK Fox & Hounds
(Maiden Newton 444)
Free House. Old-world village pub. Bar meals. Garden. Children's/family room off main entrance passage. Traditional beer.
1½m N off A356 in Maiden Newton.

96 PORTISHAM King's Arms
(Abbotsbury 342)
Devenish. Roadside pub. Large garden with hut for children.
On B3157 4m W of Weymouth.

97 WEYMOUTH Franchaise Street
Chapel Hay (W 786811)
Eldridge Pope. On top of the hill, off the beaten track, fishermen's pub. Cooked meals. Seafood speciality. Garden with swings. Use of skittle alley as family room. Traditional ale.
E. of Portland road, at top of hill.

98 OVERCOMBE (Weymouth) Embassy
** (Preston 833141)
Devenish. Modern pub off main road. Grand views over sea. Buffet and hot meals. Garden with swings. Large children's verandah.
On A353 2m NE of Weymouth.

99 PRESTON Ship (P 832115)
Devenish. Modernized roadside pub. Bar meals. Large garden with own stage. Children's room with numerous amusements. Party nights. Traditional beer.
On A353, 3m N of Weymouth.

100 OSMINGTON Sunray (Preston 832148)
** Devenish. Modern pub on main road. B & B. Restaurant, bar meals. Garden with swings etc. Children's room with amusements. Soft-drinks bar evenings in high season.
On A353 4m NE of Weymouth.

101 ANSTY Fox (Milton Abbas 880328)
* Free House. One-time private house, home of the Blandford brewers. Collection of toby jugs and plates. Accommodation. Cold buffet mornings and evenings. Garden. Children's room with games and soft-drinks bar at weekends. Traditional beer. Well worth finding.
3m E off B8143.

102 FIDDLEFORD Fiddleford
Sturminster Newton 72489)
Free House. Old brewery converted. B & B. Restaurant evenings (not Sun, Tues). Bar meals. Garden. Small games room off main bar used as family room. Traditional beer.
On A357.

103 TARRANT HINTON Crown (TH 369)
Hall & Woodhouse. Old coaching stop. B & B. Bar meals all times. Patio in front and old smithy as family room. Traditional beer.
Awkward new roundabout on A354.

104 SIXPENNY HANDLEY Roebuck
** (Handley 201)
Free House. 18th C village pub rebuilt, off beaten track. Bar meals. Garden with swings. Children's room off the garden in stable attic. Traditional beer.
On B3081 Shaftesbury/Ringwood road, 1m from A354.

105 WIMBORNE MINSTER The Square
Albion (Wimborne 882492)
Hall & Woodhouse. Old coaching station. B & B. Restaurant, meals, buffet. Garden. Children's room with soft-drinks bar (seasonal) and games.
In town centre on one-way system off A31.

106 CHURCH KNOWLE (nr Corfe Castle)
* New Inn (Corfe Castle 357)
Devenish. Off beaten track, part thatched. Restaurant (closed Sun and Mon except bank holidays). Bar meals. Large garden and children's room with games (own soft-drinks bar in high season). Skittle alley available.

MAP 2

N off A351 1m at foot of castle.

107 KINGSTON Scott Arms
(Corfe Castle 270)
Devenish. Old stone pub off main road with two car parks. B & B. Snacks in summer, bar meals in winter. Gardens and family room off main passage.
On B3069 S of Corfe Castle.

108 WORTH MATRAVERS
Square & Compass (WM 229)
Whitbread. Small off-the-beaten-track pub with fine cliff-top views. Snacks. Patio garden. Small children's room, if wet, off patio. Traditional beer.
1m S off B3069 on Isle of Purbeck.

109 LANGTON MATRAVERS
King's Arms (Swanage 2979)
Whitbread. Quaint old village pub. B & B. Snacks. Garden and children's room with TV. Traditional beer.
On B3069 2m W of Swanage.

110 LANGTON MATRAVERS Ship
(Swanage 2887)
Whitbread. Victorian pub. B & B. Snacks. Garden and family hut with TV. Traditional beer.
On B3069 2m W of Swanage.

111 SWANAGE High Street Anchor
(S 3020)
Whitbread. 17th C fishermen's pub. Beamed bars. B & B, bar snacks. Children's room off main bar.
On one-way system at end of A351.

112 SWANAGE High Street White Swan
(S 3615)
Whitbread. Typical town pub modernized. Substantial snacks. Garden (high season, soft-drinks bar). Children's room with games.
On one-way system at end of A351.

113 PARKSTONE (Poole) Parr Street
Bricklayer's Arms (P 740304)
Eldridge Pope. Off main road, Victorian pub. Hot and cold meals all day and evening. Garden with swings, and family room in old skittle alley.
Off A351 in town centre.

114 PARKSTONE (Poole) Longfleet Road
Shah of Persia (P 85462)
Eldridge Pope. A town pub. Bar meals all day and evenings. Forecourt and children's room off lounge. Traditional beer.
At crossroads on A35.

115 BOSCOMBE Christchurch Road
Salisbury Bars (Bournemouth 33478)
Eldridge Pope. A modern main-road town pub with restricted parking in side streets. Restaurant (closed Sun). Bar meals. Children's room off disco bar in basement with pool table and soft-drinks bar.
On main A35 Bournemouth/Christchurch road.

116 SOUTHBOURNE (Bournemouth)
Cranleigh Road Athelstan Arms
(Bournemouth 427601)
Eldridge Pope. Turn-of-century pub off main road. B & B. Lunches (not Sun). Garden with children's room off.
On B3059, outskirts of Bournemouth.

117 SOUTHBOURNE (Bournemouth)
Fisherman's Walk Pinecliffe
(Bournemouth 426312)
Devenish. Modern town house. Restaurant, bar meals. Live music evenings next to family room off main entrance. Traditional beer.
Off B3059, outskirts of Bournemouth, Christchurch end.

118 HIGHCLIFFE (Christchurch)
Lymington Road Globe (H 71360)
Whitbread. Old posting house. Restaurant, bar meals. Garden and patio. Family room off car park.
Off A337 Christchurch/Bournemouth road near Hengistbury Head.

119 TUCKTON Riverside (T 429210)
Whitbread. A rebuilt pub standing back from River Avon. Restaurant, bar meals. Patio at back with family room leading off.
At bridge on B3059 Christchurch/Bournemouth road.

120 ST LEONARDS Pied Piper (St L 874526)
Eldridge Pope. Modern pub on main road. Bar meals. Patio with large family room off lounge or from car park.
On A31.

121 ALDERHOLT Churchill Arms
(Fordingbridge 52147)
Hall & Woodhouse. Typical village pub in the wilds. Meals (except Tues eve). Gardens, swings, etc. Games room off the garden or from main bar. Traditional beer.
On byroad between Fordingbridge and Cranborne off B3075.

MAP 2

HAMPSHIRE (see also Map 3)

122 BURLEY   Queen's Head (B 2241)
 * Whitbread. 17th C brick pub in pictures-
 que New Forest village. Bar snacks.
 Patio with small family/children's room
 off.
 S off A31 2m E of Ringwood.

**123 NEW MILTON Christchurch Road
George** (NM 610104)
 Whitbread. Victorian main-road pub. B &
 B. Bar snacks. Small garden and family
 room off main entrance.
 On A337 in town centre.

124 SWAY   Hare & Hounds
 (Lymington 682404)
 Whitbread. One-time farm. Meals occasionally. Snacks. Garden at back. Children's room off garden alongside car park,
 with amusements.
 Off B3055 in New Forest.

125 BROCKENHURST Lyndhurst Road
 * **Rose & Crown** (B 2225)
 Eldridge Pope. Picturesque old pub on
 18th C site. B & B. Restaurant Sun and
 evenings. Buffet and bar meals. Large
 pretty gardens with family room off (and
 skittle alley in season). Traditional beer.
 In village centre.

126 FAWLEY (Holbury)   Holbury (F 891431)
 Whitbread. Red-brick main-road pub on
 outskirts of Fawley. Hot and cold meals.
 Garden with family room off, at back.
 On A326 NW of Fawley.

127 SOUTHAMPTON (Woolston)   Seaweed
 ** (S 447392)
 Free House. A modern pub, enlarged
 private house, near the Hamble River
 front. Restaurant, bar lunches, snacks.
 Garden with tables and chairs. Children's
 room with games and soft-drinks bar.
 In SE suburbs near Solent.

**128 SOUTHAMPTON (West End)
Sportsman** (West End 2570)
 Whitbread. A modern roadside pub.
 Weekday lunches. Sandwiches other
 times. Garden with swings and rounda-
 bout. Large children's room at rear.
 On NE outskirts off the A27/A33.

**129 EASTLEIGH Twyford Road
Golden Hind** (E 612583)
 Whitbread. Large mock-Tudor-fronted
 pub on main road. Lunches Mon to Fri.
 Light snacks other times. Garden at back

with family room off the garden. Traditional beer.
 In town centre.

130 WINCHESTER   Coach Station (W 2786)
 Eldridge Pope. Modern brick building in
 coach station park. Bar snacks (available
 in cafeteria as well). Family room. Patio
 at end.
 In centre of town at bus/coach station.

131 LECKFORD   Leckford Hut
 (Stockbridge 738)
 Marston. One-time drover's pub. Bar
 meals (not Mon evenings). Garden with
 amusements. Room off bar for children
 (mornings only).
 On A30 E of Stockbridge.

132 WHITCHURCH Station Road   Railway
 (W 2331)
 Whitbread. Old Victorian railway pub out
 of town. Light snacks. Garden and small
 family room (once stabling).
 Off A34 ¼m N of Whitchurch.

**133 WHITWAY (nr Newbury)
Caernarvon Arms** (Burghclere 222)
 Courage. Main-road coaching stage.
 Cold buffet. Garden. Family room off
 lounge bar with TV. Traditional beer.
 On A34 3m S of Newbury.

**134 BISHOPS WALTHAM Winchester Road
Railway** (BW 2450)
 Whitbread. One-time hotel for disused
 railway. B & B. Snacks. Small garden and
 use of dining room as family room, off
 main bar. Traditional beer.
 On A333.

135 DUNDRIDGE   Hampshire Bowman
 (Bishops Waltham 2940)
 Gales. Old farm cottages converted and
 hard to find. Bar meals hot and cold.
 Clay-pigeon shooting, archery, orchard,
 garden and patio. Stables converted for
 family room. Traditional beer.
 W off A32 1½m.

136 DROXFORD High Street   Baker's Arms
 (D 533)
 Allied. 17th C one-time bakery selling
 beer as secondary trade. B & B. Substantial snacks. Garden with slide and
 swings. Lounge off main bar for children.
 On A32 in village centre.

137 WEST MEON   Meon Hut
 Courage. Old main-road coaching

MAP 2

change house at crossroads. Restaurant, bar meals. Children's paradise in fine weather, swings, etc, own outdoor bar. Verandah shelter for the family in bad weather.
On A32/A27 crossroads.

138 SWANMORE   Hunter's Inn
* (Droxford 214)
Free House. 17th C shooting lodge off the beaten track. Substantial bar meals. Garden with swings. Small children's room off patio at back of Tavern bar. Traditional ale available.
W off A32 1½m.

139 SHEDFIELD   Black Horse
(Wickham 832300)
Allied. Old site with late Victorian brick pub. Bar snacks. Garden with swings. Children's room in converted stables.
On A333 Winchester road.

140 HAMBLE   Bugle (H 3104)

* Watneys. Said to be 12 C, an old beamed waterside pub. Restaurant, quick meals and snacks. Large garden overlooking river. Children's room off the bar.
At end of B3397 one-way street by Solent.

141 GOSPORT (Rowner) Rowner Road
Green Dragon (G 80851)
Whitbread. Modern pub in new town area. Bar meals Mon to Fri. Snacks weekends. Patio at back with family room with TV off it.
W off A32 in new centre.

142 PORTCHESTER
Somerway Lane   Seagull
(Fareham 237015)
Whitbread. Modern pub on main south-coast road. Bar meals. Small garden with family room off and adjoining public bar.
At roundabout on A27, 1m from J11 M27.

MAP 2
Other pubs to try

EAST DEVON (see also Map 1)

AXMOUTH   Ship   Play area
EXMOUTH   Exmouth Arms   Children's facilities
EXMOUTH   Volunteer   Children's facilities
KILMINGTON   New Inn   Play area
LADRAM BAY   Three Rocks   Children's facilities
MILMINGTON   New Inn   Play area
OTTERTON   Red Lion   Children's facilities
OTTERY ST MARY   Salston   Own grounds
ROCKBEARE   Bidgood Arms   Children's facilities
SAMPFORD PEVERELL   Farmhouse Inn   Patio and play area
STOCKLAND   Kings Arms   Play area and children's facilities
TOPSHAM   Passage   Riverside
UPOTTERY   Sidmouth Arms   Play area and children's facilities

SOMERSET

APPLEY   Globe   Rambling gardens
BATCOMBE   Three Horseshoes   Garden
BATHPOOL   Creech Castle   Own grounds
BICKNOLLER   Bicknoller   Play area
BLAGDON HILL (nr Blagdon)   Holman Clavel   Garden, play area and views
BREAN   Brean Down   Play area
BRENT KNOLL   Red Cow   Play area
BURROW BRIDGE   King Alfred   Garden and waterside
CANNINGTON   Blue Anchor   Waterside garden and play area
CASTLE CARY   Britannia   Children's facilities
CHARD   George   Children's facilities
COMBWICH   Anchor   Waterside play area
CRANMORE   Strode Arms   Garden, play area and duck pond
CUDWORTH   Windwhistle   Play area. Near Cricket St Thomas Wild Life Park

MAP 2

ENMORE   **Enmore**   Play area
EVERCREECH   **Pecking Mill**   Children's facilities
HENSTRIDGE   **Virginia Ash**   Large garden and play area
HUNTWORTH   **Boat & Anchor**   Waterside
LANGFORD BUDVILLE   **Martlet**   Garden and play area
LONG SUTTON   **Lime Kiln**   Play area
MELLS   **Talbot**   Children's facilities and garden play area
MOORLAND   **Thatchers**   Waterside
PAWLETT   **Manor**   Own grounds
POLSHAM   **Blue Bowl**   Play area
PRIDDY   **New Inn**   Village green
QUEEN CAMEL   **Mildmay Arms**   Children's facilities
RODE   **Red Lion**   Children's facilities
RODNEY STOKE   **Rodney Stoke**   Children's facilities and garden
RUSHINGTON (Taunton)   **Black Brook**   Play area
SPARKFORD   **Sparkford**   Play area and children's facilities
STOKE-SUB-HAMDON   **Prince of Wales**   Children's facilities
TEMPLECOMBE   **Royal**   Swings
TYTHERINGTON   **Fox & Hounds**   Play area, nr Longleat
UPTON NOBLE   **Lamb**   Garden with views
WEST COKER   **Royal George**   Play area and swings
WEST QUANTOXHEAD   **Windmill**   Play area
WHATLEY   **Sun Inn**   Garden with swings
WOOKEY   **Ring o' Bells**   Play area
WRANTAGE   **Canal**   Waterside garden
YEOVIL   **Great Western**   Children's facilities
YEOVIL   **Picketty Witch**   Garden and swings

AVON

BATH   **Park Tavern**   Garden with children's bar
BATHAMPTON   **George**   Waterside
BLAGDON   **New Inn**   Lakeside gardens and views
BRISTOL (Prince Street)   **Shakespeare**   Quayside
HINTON BLEWETT   **Ring o' Bells**   Village green
KEWSTOKE   **Commodore**   Waterside
LOCKING   **Coach House**   Play area
NEWTON ST LOE   **Globe**   Play area
PENSFORD   **Traveller's Rest**   Play area
PORTISHEAD   **Hole in One**   Sea views and play area
REDHILL   **Bung**   Play area
RIDGEHILL   **Crown**   Play area and views
SALTFORD   **Jolly Sailor**   Waterside and play area
WORLE   **Night Jar**   Play area
YATTON   **White Horse**   Views and play area

GLOUCESTERSHIRE (see also Map 5)

AYLBURTON (nr Lydney)   **Cross**   Children's facilities
FOREST GREEN   **Jovial Foresters**   Children's facilities and garden
FRAMPTON MANSELL (nr Stroud)   **White Horse Inn**   Swings
KEMPSFORD   **George**   Garden and swings
LECHLADE   **Trout**   Waterside garden
ULEY   **King's Head**   Children's facilities

OXFORDSHIRE (see also Maps 3 & 5)

ABINGDON   **Nag's Head**   Riverside

MAP 2

ABINGDON (Oxford Road)   Ox   Swings and slide
ASTON   Bull   Swings etc
CHILDREY (nr Wantage)   Hatchett   Playground
DENCHWORTH   Fox   Playground
FRILFORD HEATH (Nr Abingdon)   Dog House   Trampoline
GORING   Old Leathern Bottle   Riverside with moorings
GROVE (nr Wantage)   Bay Tree   Playground
LETCOMBE REGIS (nr Wantage)   Sparrow   Playground
LONG WITTENHAM   Plough   Riverside with moorings
NORTHMOOR   Dun Cow   Aviary
RADLEY (nr Abingdon)   Bowyer Arms   Play area and children's shop
SHIPPON (nr Abingdon)   Prince of Wales   Swings, slide and roundabout
SHRIVENHAM   Bearring Arms   Aviary and garden
STANDLAKE   Bell   Garden and camping
STEVENTON   King's Arms   Play area and aviary
UPTON (nr Didcot)   George & Dragon   Playground and aviary
WANTAGE (Charlton Road)   Lord Nelson   Playground

BERKSHIRE (see also Map 3)

BEEDON   Coach & Horses   Swings and climbing frame
CHEVELEY   Red Lion   Garden play area
DONNINGTON (nr Newbury)   Donnington Castle   Garden and play area
GREAT SHEFFORD   Swan   Waterside patio and garden
HUNGERFORD   Bear   Children's facilities and garden
KINTBURY   Dundas Arms   Canalside
PANGBOURNE   Cross Keys   Riverside

WILTSHIRE

BERWICK ST JOHN   Talbot   Swings and Wendy house
CHOLDERTON   Crown Inn   Garden, swings, goats and pony
CRUDWELL   Plough   Children's facilities and garden
DONHEAD   Rising Sun   Garden with swings
HORNINGSHAM   Bath Arms   Garden and green
KINGSTON ST MICHAEL   Plough   Play area, picnic area alongside, J17 M4
MELKSHAM   Bear   Children's facilities and garden
MERE   Walnut Tree   Swings
STEEPLE LANGFORD   Rainbow's End   Garden overlooking lakes
SWINDON (Redcliffe Street)   Even Swindon   Children's facilities and garden
WANBOROUGH   Brewers Arms   Garden, aviary and animals
WINGFIELD   Poplars   Garden and cricket square
WOODFORD   Bridge   Garden and swings
WOODFORD   Wheatsheaf   Large playground and children's bar
WOOTTON BASSETT   Salley Pussey   Swings, garden, slide
WROUGHTON   Swan   Children's facilities and garden

DORSET

ABBOTSBURY   Swan   Play area
ALLINGTON (nr Bridport)   Boot   Children's facilities
ALLINGTON (nr Bridport)   White Lion   Children's facilities
ASHLEY HEATH   Struan Arms   Large play area and garden
BEAMINSTER   Sun Inn   Children's facilities
BOURTON   Red Lion   Swings and mineral bar
BRIDPORT   Lord Nelson   Children's facilities
BRIDPORT   Màson's Arms   Children's facilities
BRIDPORT   Toll House   Children's facilities

MAP 2

BRIDPORT (West Bay Road) **Crown** Play area
CASHMOOR **Cashmoor** Play area
CHARMINSTER **New Inn** Pets' corner, covered patio
CHARMOUTH **George** Children's facilities
CHEDDINGTON **Wynyards Gap** Views and play area
COLEHILL **Barley Mow** Playground and mineral bar
COLEHILL (Furze Hill) **Stocks** Garden and play area
CORFE MULLEN (nr Wimborne) **Dorset Soldier** See-saw etc
CRANBORNE **Fleur de Lys** Swings and slides
EAST CHALDON **Sailor's Return** Play area
EASTON (Portland) **Punch Bowl** Children's facilities
GODMANSTONE **Smith's Arms** England's smallest pub. Garden and stream
HOLLYWELL **Strangways** Children's facilities
KING'S STAG **Green Man** Commonside, play area
KINSON **Thatched House** Play area
LULWORTH **Castle** Children's facilities, garden, play area
LYME REGIS (The Cob) **Royal Standard** On seafront
MARNHULL **Crown** Skittle alley and play area
PAMPHILL (nr Wimborne) **Vine** Open-air draughtsboard
PIDDLEHINTON **Thimble** Swings and pets' corner
POOLE **Night Jar** Play area (summer only)
PUDDLETOWN **Prince of Wales** Playground
SEATON (nr Chideock) **Anchor** Children's facilities, beach and fossils
SHAFTESBURY **Half Moon** Garden, play area
SHAPWICK **Anchor Inn** Swings
SHILLINGSTONE **Seymour Arms** Swings
STANDPIT (nr Christchurch) **Ship in Distress** Play area
SWANAGE **Black Swan** Children's facilities in outbuilding with colour TV
SWANAGE **Red Lion** Children's facilities in converted outhouse
TOLPUDDLE **Martyrs** Swings
TRENT **Rose & Crown** Historic pub with play area and skittle alley
VERWOOD **Albion** Garden and aviary
VERWOOD **Monmouth Ash** Playground
WEST BAY (nr Bridport) **Bridport Arms** Children's facilities
WEYMOUTH **Golden Lion** Children's facilities
WEYMOUTH **Northey Tavern** Views over harbour
WIMBORNE MINSTER **Green Man** Play area and facilities sometimes
WIMBORNE ST GILES **Bull Inn** Swings and slides
WINFRITH **Red Lion** Play area
WINTERBOURNE KINGSTON **Greyhound** Swings and pets' corner
WINTON (nr Bournemouth) **Bear** Swings

HAMPSHIRE (see also Map 3)

ALRESFORD **Globe** Waterside
AVON (nr Christchurch) **Tyrrells Ford** Lawns and gardens
BUCKLER'S HARD **Master Builders** Waterside, gardens and children's facilities
BURLEY **White Buck** Lawns and garden, daytime children's facilities
CADNAM **Sir John Barleycorn** Commonside, play area (start of M27)
CHERITON (nr Alresford) **Jolly Farmer** Aviary, peacock
CURBRIDGE **Horse & Jockey** Riverside garden
DEANE **Deane Gate** Garden and children's facilities
EASTLEIGH **Prince of Wales** Riverside garden and children's facilities
EXTON **Shoe Inn** Garden and aviary
FORDINGBRIDGE **George** Riverside garden
GRATELY **Plough Inn** Swings and slides
HATCH (Basingstoke) **Hatch** Children's facilities and play area (J6 M3)
HIGHTOWN (nr Ringwood) **Elm Tree** Children's facilities and play area
HORDLE **Folly** Commonside and children's facilities
KINGS WORTHY **Cart & Horses** Children's play area

MAP 2

LINWOOD **Red Shoot** Shop, village green and large patio
LITTLEDOWN (nr Vernham Street) **Boot** Views and play area
LYMINGTON **May Pole** Large waterside garden
LYNDHURST **Waterloo** Garden play area
MARTIN **Coote Arms** Playground
MICHELDEVER **Luneways** Garden play area
MINSTEAD **Trusty Servant** Village green
NORTH WALTHAM **Wheatsheaf** Children's facilities (J8 M3)
OWER **Vine** Children's facilities and play area
PAMBER **Queen's College Arms** Garden and play area
PORTSDOWN **Churchillian** Play area, commonside, views
RINGWOOD **Fish** Riverside garden
ROCKFORD **Alice Lisle** Commonside, play area
ROMSEY **Duke's Head** Waterside garden
SOPLEY **Woolpack** Riverside garden, play area
SOUTHAMPTON (Woolston) **Gardener's Arms** Swings
SPARSHOLT **Plough Inn** Children's facilities in old barn with own bar
STUBBINGTON **Swordfish** Large garden, play area
THRUXTON **White Horse** Garden and play area
TIMSBURY **Malt House** Children's facilities in hut with amusements and soft-drinks
bar
WARNFORD **George Inn** Riverside
WHITSBURY **Cartwheel** Children's facilities, garden, play area
WHERWELL **White Lion** Swings and see-saw
WINKTON **Fisherman's Haunt** Garden, patio, amusements, play area

ISLE OF WIGHT

ARRETON **White Lion** Children's facilities in old stable
BEMBRIDGE **Row Barge** Children's facilities in old snooker room
BRIGHSTONE **Three Bishops** Children's facilities and garden
GODSHILL **Griffin** Children's facilities and garden
NEWPORT **White Lion** Family cabin
NEWPORT (Park Cross) **Blacksmiths Arms** Children's facilities, books and toys
NINGWOOD **Horse & Groom** Children's facilities in two huts
NITON **Royal Sandrock** Children's facilities and garden
ST HELENS **Ferry Boat Inn** Overlooking Bembridge harbour
SANDOWN **Castle** Children's facilities
SANDOWN **Commercial** Children's facilities
SHANKLIN **Crab Inn** Play area, play room
VENTNOR **Royal** Children's facilities and garden

MAP 3

HAMPSHIRE (see also Map 2)

**1 SOUTHSEA (Portsmouth) Grenada Road
Grenada** (Portsmouth 20350)
Whitbread. Usual 1930s building. Lunches (Mon to Sat). Snacks other times.
Patio. Covered courtyard, cold in winter.
Near shopping centre.

2 PETERSFIELD   Welcome Inn (P 5156)
Whitbread. Large modern main-road pub.
Bar meals. Small patio with children's
room off it and the car park.
On A3 in town centre.

3 ALTON Market Square   Wheatsheaf
(A 83316)
Courage. One-time coaching stage,
many uses since. Public car park in market. Lunches Mon to Fri. Snacks other
times. Large dining room used as family
room. Traditional beer.
Just off town centre. Market Square
one-way street.

4 FLEET   Fleet (F 4839)
Allied. Victorian railway hotel. B & B.
Restaurant. Bar snacks. Garden. swings.
Pool room off car park for families. TV
room upstairs. Traditional beer.
Just off A323 by railway station.

5 HARTLEY WINTNEY   Swan (HW 2101)
Allied. Old coaching stage on A30. Restaurant (not Sat morning, Sun eve, Mon
all day). Bar meals. Buffet. Patio, garden.
Family room off restaurant. Traditional
beer.
On A30 in village centre. 3m from J5 M3.

BERKSHIRE (see also Map 2)

6 ETON WICK Common Road   Greyhound
(Windsor 63925)
Courage. Small village local, hard to find.
Snacks, patio. Children's room with
games in old stables off car park. Traditional beer.
1½m from Windsor, off B3026 in village
side road.

**7 LITTLEWICK GREEN Bath Road
Shire Horse** (LG 53351)
Courage. A modern pub. Restaurant, bar
meals. Patio. Shire Horse centre alongside with gardens, shops, aviaries and
tea room used as family room for pub
(closes 5 pm). The whole centre is being
reorganised and rebuilt 1980-81. Traditional beer.

W on A4, ½m from A423M spur of M4
(J8/9).

HERTFORDSHIRE (see also Map 6)

**8 LONG   MARSTON   Tring   Road   Old
Queen's Head** (Cheddington 668368)
ABC. One-time butcher's shop and
smallholding. Lunches Mon to Fri.
Snacks w/ends and evenings. Garden
with swings and family room with TV
and games. Traditional beer.
2½m W of Tring, in village.

9 CHIPPERFIELD The Green   Two Brewers
(Kings Langley 65266)
Free House. Famous old house, was cottages converted. Accommodation. Restaurant. Bar meals. Patio. Families may
use lounge overlooking green. Traditional
beer.
N off A404 at Chorley Wood, in village
centre.

**10 CROXLEY GREEN (nr Watford)
The Green   Artichoke**
(Rickmansworth 72565)
Allied. Georgian brick-built pub on village
green. Snacks. Garden. Family room off
garden and saloon bar. Traditional beer.
Off A432 on long green.

**11 HALLS GREEN (Weston) nr Baldock
** Rising Sun** (Weston 236)
McMullen. Small 17th C one-time smallholding off the beaten track. Bar meals
up to 9 pm daily. Large garden with birds
and games. Family room in garden with
games. Traditional beer.
W off B1037 1m.

ESSEX (see also Map 6)

**12 WALTHAM ABBEY Highbridge Street
Old English Gentleman** (WA 718723)
McMullen. Old bargees' pub on canal
bank. Garden with open verandah at side
for children. Cold in winter.
On link road between A10 and A11.

**13 MATCHING TYE   Hare & Hounds
*** (M 274)
Courage. Typical Victorian village pub on
the green. Roadside parking. Bar meals.
Garden with animals and shop. Family
room with amusements in garden. Traditional beer.
On B183 E of Harlow in village.

MAP 3

14 BLACKMORE Church Street   Bull
(B 821208)
Allied. 14th C church house then coaching change. Restaurant (not Mon eve). Bar meals. Garden with swings and slide. Small children's room off car park. Traditional beer.
S off A122 in village.

15 BATTLESBRIDGE   Barge
(Wickford 2662)
Allied. Quaint old character pub. Bar meals. Garden with games. Family room off main entrance. Traditional beer.
On A132, 3m N of Basildon.

16 CANVEY ISLAND Knightswyck Road
Oyster Fleet (CI 2318)
Free House. First private brick-built house on the Island. Restaurant. Lunches Mon-Sat. Bar meals other times. Garden with lake with birds. Seesaw and frame. Small family room in entrance hall. Traditional beer.
In town centre on one-way street.

17 SOUTHEND Marine Parade   Hope
(S 67413)
Watneys. Old Victorian pub overlooking the sea and pier. Restricted parking. B & B. Large family room off main entrance (also overlooking sea).
At end of A13 on sea front.

18 SOUTHCHURCH Wakering Road   Rose
(Southend 588008)
Watneys. One-time farmhouse. Buffet and bar meals. Garden with family room off. Traditional beer.
Off A13 2m N of Southend.

19 GREAT WAKERING 23 High Street
Anchor (Southend 219265)
Bass. Rebuilt turn of the century on site of fishing cottage. Small restaurant, bar meals (seafood speciality). Patio. Stable converted for family room with games and soft-drinks bar. Traditional beer.
On B1017 in village centre.

20 SOUTHMINSTER Station Road   Railway
(Maldon 772206)
Grays. Quaint old Victorian pub outside and in. Roadside parking. Pies available. Lounge used as family room, off the main entrance hall. Traditional beer.
On B1021 1m N of Burnham-on-Crouch.

21 TILLINGHAM   Swan (T 210)
Free House. Mock Tudor country pub. B & B. Bar meals and snacks. Garden with swings and slide. Family room off main passage from garden.
On B1021 4m N of Burnham-on-Crouch.

22 GREAT LEIGHS   Dog & Partridge
(GL 331)
Ridleys. One-time farm cottage. Bar meals. Garden and small children's room with games. TV at back between the bars. Traditional beer.
On A131.

23 BRAINTREE Rayne Road
Horse & Groom (B 23362)
Allied. One-time coaching posting house. B & B. Snacks. Garden. Covered verandah (cold in winter), popular family room off car park. Traditional beer.
On A131 in town centre.

24 COLCHESTER East Gates
Rose & Crown (C 76677)
Free House. 16th C timber-framed town house. Accommodation. Restaurant. Bar meals. Children can use foyer and part of bar entrance. Traditional beer.
In town centre.

GREATER LONDON

25 SOUTHWARK SE1   George
(01-407-2056)
Whitbread. National Trust. Famous old minstrel gallery in coaching inn. Restaurant. Bar meals. Large courtyard. Upstairs balcony for children. Traditional beer.
On A2 S of London Bridge.

26 BANKSIDE (Southwark SE1)   Anchor
(01-407-1577)
Courage. Famous waterside pub. Restaurant, bar meals, large viewing platform overlooking Thames. Family room off west end of pub entrance.
In back streets between Southwark Bridge/Blackfriars Bridge.

27 HAMMERSMITH W6 (19 Upper Mall)
Doves (01-748-5405)
Fuller, Smith & Turner. Famous Georgian riverside house of character. Buffet & bar meals. Restricted roadside parking nearby. Back covered all-weather verandah and patio overlooking river. Traditional beer.
Make for Hammersmith pier W. of Hammersmith Bridge. By foot in alleyway.

28 STREATHAM Greyhound Lane
** **Greyhound** (01-677-9962)

MAP 3

Watneys. Old coaching house rebuilt, just off main road. Substantial bar meals, home cooking (not Sun or evenings). Snacks other times. Garden. Family verandah off garden and main bar.
On A23/217 junction on common.

SURREY

29 WALTON-ON-THAMES Towpath, Sunbury Lane Weir (W 54530)
Courage. Mock Tudor riverside pub. Restaurant, buffet lunches and dinners. Large riverside gardens and own moorings, 100ft landing stage. Loggia where children may be left to romp in wet weather and winter.
Off the B370 1m E of Walton, down the Towpath.

30 HAMBLEDON Merry Harriers (Wormley 2883)
Allied. 16th C farmhouse enlarged. Bar snacks. Garden with swings and frames. Family room off main bar with pool table. Traditional beer.
Off A283 on edge of village.

31 GODALMING Meadrow Railway (G 6680)
Courage. Victorian railway hotel. Bar meals. Patio. Large hall at back used as family room. Traditional beer.
Off A3100.

32 GOMSHALL Black Horse (Shere 2242)
Youngs. One-time brewery and offices. B & B. Restaurant (except Sun eve, Mon all day). Bar meals. Picturesque garden. Main entrance hall used as children's room. Traditional beer.
Off A25 in village centre.

33 EFFINGHAM Forest Road Lord Howard (E Horsley 2572)
Allied. Modern red-brick pub on old site. Lunches Mon-Fri (children's portions). Good bar snacks. Garden with swings, etc. Large family room off lounge entrance with amusements. Traditional ale.
Off A246 in village centre.

34 GREAT BOOKHAM High Street Old Crown (Bookham 58119)
Courage. Rebuilt pub on old site. Lunches Mon-Fri. Snacks other times except Sun. Garden with swings and family room off it and the lounge bar. Traditional beer.
N off A246 in village centre.

35 BANSTEAD Park Road Mint (Burgh Heath 58538)
Bass. Quaint old bar, hard to find, once a blacksmith's. Buffet (not Sun). Snacks other times. Garden. Small children's room off bar. Traditional beer.
S off main village street.

36 CATERHAM Stanstead Road Harrow
* (C 43260)
Allied. Character country pub. Substantial bar meals except Sun morn. Children's portions. Garden with amusements. Family room with amusements for wet weather and winter. Traditional beer.
In village off Church Hill 1½m from station.

37 CHURT Tilford Road Pride of the Valley (Hindhead 5799)
Free House. Old farmhouse on edge of Lloyd George's estate. Restaurant. Accommodation. Bar meals. Garden. Use of lounge for families. Traditional beer.
On A289 N of Hindhead.

WEST SUSSEX

38 MIDHURST North Street Angel (M 2421)
Gales. An old coaching house in town centre. Coachyard car park. Accommodation. Restaurant. A fine old walled garden behind the coaching yard. Foyer where children may be left. Traditional beer.
On A286 in town centre.

39 COCKING CAUSEWAY (nr Midhurst) Greyhound (Midhurst 3300)
Gales. One-time farm cottage on main A287 Chichester Road. Lunches Mon-Sat. Snacks other times. Garden. Family room in old cottage in garden. Traditional beer. Coaches welcome.
On A286 1m S of Midhurst.

40 COCKING Blue Bell
Whitbreads. Coaching change house on A287. Bar meals. Garden. Children's room off main entrance.
On A286 in village. S of Midhurst.

41 CHIDHAM Old House at Home (Bosham 572477)
Free House. Quaint old cottages converted. Bar meals. Garden play area and new home brewery. Family room off

MAP 3

main bar with games. Traditional beer.
S off A27 1m. 3m W of Chichester.

42 SIDLESHAM (nr Chichester)
Jolly Fisherman
Allied. Small village pub on main road.
Snacks. Garden. Small children's room
(open May-October).
On B2145 S of Chichester.

43 ELMER   Cabin
Free House. A modern pub, 3 mins from
sea. Snacks available daytime and evenings. Patio in front and large well-organ-
ised children's room with games.
S off A259 through Middleton.

44 YAPTON   Shoulder   of   Mutton   &
Cucumbers (Y 551429)
Watneys. The longest pub name in
Britain. Roadside parking. Lunches
weekdays, bar snacks weekends. Small
children's room off the bar with entry to
garden.
N off A2024 W of Littlehampton.

45 FORD   Ship & Anchor (Yapton 551747)
Free House. Riverside farm converted.
Restaurant, bar meals, garden with
amusements. Camping. Games room
available for children.
N off A27, signed Ford Junction. ½m up
from driveway.

46 DEVIL'S DYKE (Brighton)   Devil's Dyke
(Poynings 256)
Bass. Beauty spot with views. Restaurant, cafe, patio and fields. Large entrance porch and cafe for children.
Follow Dyke road from Brighton to con-
clusion.

47 COPSALE (nr Horsham)   Bridge House
(Southwater 730383)
King & Barnes. A small village pub.
Snacks available lunchtime, limited
evenings. Small room at back for child-
ren, off garden. Traditional beer.
E off A24.

48 SLAUGHAM   Chequers (Handcross 239)
Free House. Victorian village local on
village green. Roadside parking. Snacks
at lunchtime. Patio for fine days and club
room all year round (or cellar on Sundays). Traditional beer.
W off A23 S of Crawley.

49 SLINFOLD (nr Horsham)   King's Head
(S 790339)
Whitbread. An old village pub, Georgian

in origin. Roadside parking. Lunches in
bar and evening meals in dining room
(except Sun and Mon). Small family
room at back leading to garden.
Off A264 in village W of Horsham.

50 RUSPER (Horsham) Friday Street
Royal Oak (R 393)
King & Barnes. A small, isolated, hard-to-
find pub. Bar meals and snacks. Garden,
play area. Verandah for families. Tradi-
tional beer.
Between Rusper and Capel, S to
Horsham 3m.

EAST SUSSEX

51 FOREST ROW London Road
Brambletye (FR 2575)
Free House. Private house converted.
Restaurant. Lunches. Rambling bar with
foyer for children who behave. Tradi-
tional beer.
Off A22 in village centre.

52 FLETCHING   Grifffin (Newick 2890)
Free House. 17th C coaching house in
picturesque village. Lunches and evening
meals. Garden. Family/children's room
off main bar.
In village centre W off A272.

53 ISFIELD   Laughing Fish (I 399)
Beard. The old station hotel converted.
Snacks. Small garden. Small children's
room. Traditional beer.
Off A22 in village centre.

54 BERWICK STREET   Berwick
(Alfriston 870859)
Free House. Originally built as railway
hotel. Bar meals and snacks available.
Playground with adventure course and
children's room. Traditional beer.
N off A27 on B2108 1m.

55 MAYFIELD Main Street   Middle House
(M 2146)
Free House. Fine old Elizabethan man-
sion. Accommodation. Restaurant.
Large entrance porch and fine old garden
at rear available for children. Traditional
beer.
On A267 in village centre.

56 HAILSHAM   Crown (H 840041)
Courage. An old coaching house. Coaching yard. Restaurant, lunches, dinners,
snacks. Two rooms available for families
with children.

MAP 3

E off A22 in town centre on one-way system.

57 HOLLINGTON (St Leonards)
Wishing Tree
Whitbread. Quaint old pub, out of town on new housing estate. Snacks. Patio. Garden. Use of games room as family room.
E of town in new housing area.

58 HASTINGS The Ridge
Robert de Mortain (H 751061)
Whitbread. A private house on the downs overlooking Hastings. Lunches and snacks daily. Garden at back and children's room by entrance hall.
On loop road skirting N of town.

59 NORTHIAM   Six Bells (N 2110)
Free House. Rebuilt on old coaching house site. Limited parking. Snacks. Small patio. Games room for families. Traditional beer.
On A28 in village centre.

60 RYE Gun Garden   Ypres Castle (R 3248)
Whitbread. A small old pub alongside the castle. Snacks only. Garden in castle keep. Children's room alongside bars (with glass windows to keep watch). Traditional beer.
Off A259 skirting town.

61 CAMBER   Camber Castle
Free House. A modern pub near the famous sands, 2 mins walk. Bar meals daily. Games room at back with children's own toilets.
On B2075 coast road in Sand Dunes holiday village.

KENT

62 NEWCHURCH Romney Marsh
Black Bull (Dymchurch 2161)
Shepherd Neame. 17th C smuggling pub, hard to find. Roadside parking. Snacks. Garden. Family room off main passage opposite bar. Traditional beer.
W off A259 in hamlet.

63 DYMCHURCH Rye Road   Ocean
Courage. Mock Tudor with 1733 over door, backing on sea, 2 mins walk through car park. Lunches weekdays. Bar snacks. Children's room with games.
On A259 in town main road.

64 BROADSTAIRS Harbour Street

Neptune's Hall (Thanet 61400)
Shepherd Neame. Old sailors' haunt in narrow street. Car park nearby. B & B. Snacks. Yard at back, part covered, with games. Traditional beer.
In narrow one-way streets.

65 BROADSTAIRS Albion Street   Balmoral
* (B 61292)
Free House. Small Victorian pub overlooking sea. Restricted parking. Sandwiches. Small children's alcove off main bar. Traditional beer.
In narrow one-way streets.

66 HERNE BAY Station Road   Heron
(HB 2990)
Shepherd Neame. Modern brick pub. Salads, bar meals lunchtime. Snacks evenings. Small garden and family room off main entrance. Traditional beer.
Off A299 near railway station.

67 HERNE BAY Western Esplanade
Hampton (HB 4576)
Shepherd Neame. Victorian house right on the sea front. Unrestricted roadside parking. Bar snacks. Patio. Large family room with games overlooking sea off main bar. Traditional ale.
Off A299 on west end of sea front.

68 DUNKIRK (nr Faversham)   Gate
(Boughton 284)
Free House. One-time turnpike toll house, now on edge of service area. Bar meals and snacks. Children's room off car park.
On A2 dual carriageway.

69 DARGATE (nr Faversham)   Dove
Shepherd Neame. A true farm cottage in picturesque village. Limited snacks. Garden. Large family room at back of garden.
E off A299 3m from J7 M2 (Thanet Way).

70 BOUGHTON STREET   Queen's Head
(Boughton 369)
Shepherd Neame. 17th C character village pub. B & B. Bar meals (except Sat and Sun lunch). Snacks evenings. Garden. Use of Buffs room for families (except Tues and Thurs eve). Traditional beer.
S of J7 M2 on old A2.

71 OSPRINGE (nr Faversham)   Anchor
(Faversham 20850)
Shepherd Neame. One-time coaching change. Roadside parking. B & B.

Snacks. Garden. Room off back bar used as family room (or Darts room off passageway). Traditional beer.
2m from J6 M2 W of Faversham on old A2.

72 FAVERSHAM St Mary's Road
Royal William (F 2198)
Shepherd Neame. Victorian back-street pub with roadside parking. Bar snacks. Meeting-room off main bar used as family room. Traditional ale.
Off A2, 2m from J6 M2 in town-centre side-road.

73 SITTINGBOURNE Charlotte Street
Foresters' Arms (S 72183)
Whitbread. Victorian back-street pub. Roadside parking. Snacks. Family games room off main bar. Traditional beer.
N off A2 in town near Bowaters Paper Factory.

74 MINSTER (Isle of Sheppey) Chequers Road   British Queen
Shepherd Neame. Typical late-Victorian village pub. Snacks. Small garden. Family room off main bar. Traditional beer.
Off B2008 in village.

75 OAD STREET (nr Borden)
Plough & Harrow (Newington 843351)
Free House. Small Victorian building in hamlet. Lunches Mon to Fri. (No food other times unless booked.) Family room off garden. Traditional beer.
S of J5 M2 off A249 in hamlet.

76 RAINHAM Hawthorne Avenue
Dew Drop (Medway 32173)
Shepherd Neame. Modern brick pub. Bar snacks and small garden. Children's room off public bar. Traditional beer.
N off A2 in new housing estate.

77 CHATHAM Albert Road   Edward VII
(Medway 44858)
Courage. Victorian pub off the back streets. Roadside parking. Snacks. Small children's room off main bar with TV.
In town centre between A2 and A229.

78 UPPER UPNOR High Street
King's Arms (Medway 77490)
Courage. Victorian pub by old castle to protect Medway from Dutch. Bar snacks. Garden with bat and trap, and horseshoe quoits. Games room off public bar for use of families. Traditional beer.
Off A228 N of Strood towards Chatham.

79 BURHAM (nr Rochester)   Royal Albert
(Medway 666716)
Shepherd Neame. Typical village local off the main routes. Restricted parking. Light snacks. Small garden/patio and small family room off saloon bar. Traditional beer.
Between the Mid Kent motorways, E of A228.

80 STAPLEHURST   South Eastern
(S 891205)
Whitbread. Victorian main-road pub. Restaurant. Bar and buffet meals. Beer garden and use of dining room for families.
On A229 in village centre.

81 SEAL (Stone Stream)   Rose & Crown
* (Flaxted 233)
Whitbread. Old foresters' cottage off the beaten track. Bar snacks (not Sun). Garden with swings. Lodge room off public bar entrance used as family room. Traditional beer.
N off A25 E of Sevenoaks, in small hamlet and maze of roads.

MAP 3
Other pubs to try

HAMPSHIRE (see also Map 2)

BURITON   Maple   Children's facilities and garden
CHALTON (nr Petersfield)   Red Lion   Village green and garden
EAST MEON   George   Play area
EVERSLEY CROSS   Chequers   Village green
EWSHOT   Windmill   Garden with putting green
HAYLING ISLAND (Ferry Road)   Ferry Boat   Waterside
MINLEY   Crown & Cushion   Cricket green

MAP 3

BERKSHIRE (see also Map 2)

BURGHFIELD Cunning Man Canalside
COOKHAM DEAN Jolly Farmer Play area
HOLYPORT Belgian Arms Village green
OLD WINDSOR Wheatsheaf Children's facilities and garden
READING Caversham Bridge Riverside gardens
SWALLOWFIELD Crown Play area
WINDSOR Thames Riverside
WINDSOR Windsor Lad Alongside racecourse
WOKINGHAM Two Poplars Play area and aviary
WOODLEY George Riverside

OXFORDSHIRE (see also Maps 2 & 5)

ASTON ROWANT Lambert Arms Children's facilities and garden
BINFIELD HEATH Coach & Horses Play area
CANE END Fox Large playground
CHINNOR Bird in Hand Swings etc
HENLEY-ON-THAMES Angel Riverside and garden, moorings
KIDMORE END New Inn Common and pond
SATWELL Lamb Birds and animals
TETSWORTH Swan Children's facilities and garden
THAME Abingdon Arms Children's facilities and garden
WARBOROUGH Six Bells Village green
WHITCHURCH Ferry Boat Waterside

BUCKINGHAMSHIRE (see also Maps 5 & 6)

CHESHAM Pheasant Waterside
COOKHAM Ferry Riverside
COOKHAM Kings Arms Large attractive gardens
GREAT MISSENDEN Red Lion Children's facilities, garden, play area
HIGH WYCOMBE Flint Cottage Attractive garden
HOLMER GREEN Bat & Ball Commonside
IBSTONE Fox Commonside
LITTLE MARLOW Queens Head Garden and play area
LITTLE MISSENDEN Full Moon Garden and play area
PENN Squirrel Garden and village green
PRESTWOOD Pole Cat Garden and play area
TAPLOW Feathers Commonside

BEDFORDSHIRE (see also Map 6)

DUNSTABLE Chiltern Garden and indoor facilities
DUNSTABLE First & Last Swings
LEIGHTON BUZZARD Crown Garden and indoor facilities
LUTON Fountain Indoor facilities
LUTON Griffin Indoor facilities

HERTFORDSHIRE (see also Map 6)

ASTON (nr Stevenage) Pig & Whistle Attractive garden
BOXMOOR (Hemel Hempstead) Fishery Canalside
BROXBOURNE Crown Riverside garden with boats available
BULBOURNE (Tring) Lock & Quay Canalside
COLLIERS END Lamb & Flag Children's facilities and garden

MAP 3

ELSTREE **Edgwarebury** Landscaped gardens
HARPENDEN (East Common) **Three Horseshoes** Garden and pony
HATFIELD **Wrestlers** Roadhouse garden, play area
HERTFORD **Old Barge** Canalside garden
PARK STREET (St Albans) **Old Red Lion** Riverside and play area
REDBOURN **Cricketers** On common
ST ALBANS **White Lion** Garden and play area
THUNDRIDGE **Windmill** Children's facilities and garden
WALTHAM CROSS **Plough** Play area and aviary
WHEATHAMPSTEAD **Abbot John** Play area
WHEATHAMPSTEAD **Cherry Tree** Swings and play area

ESSEX (see also Map 6)

BUCKHURST HILL **Railway** Garden and indoor facilities
CHELMSFORD **Clock House** Swings, frame, playground
COLCHESTER **Maypole** Barn and kiddie rides
FYFIELD **Black Bull** Children's facilities and garden
HATFIELD HEATH **Stag** On village green
MALDON **Queen's Head** Quayside
NAVESTOCK SIDE **Green Man** Village green
NORTH FAMBRIDGE **Ferry Boat** Riverside
PURFLEET **Royal** Riverside
PURLEIGH **Bell** Panoramic estuary views
RAYLEIGH **Paul Pry** Large children's play area
SOUTHMINSTER **Railway** Children's facilities
TILBURY **World's End** Riverside
WALTHAM ABBEY **Angel** Children's facilities and garden
WICKFORD (Runwell) **Runwell Hall** Large gardens and lawns
WOODFORD BRIDGE **Crown & Crooked Billet** Village green

GREATER LONDON

BARNES (SW13 Lonsdale Road) **Bull's Head** Riverside
BARNES (SW13) **Sun** Bowling green and common
BARNES (SW13) **White Hart** Riverside garden
BATTERSEA **Old Swan** Riverside patio
CARSHALTON **Greyhound** Garden and village pond
CHELSEA (SW3) **Australian** Patio
CHELSEA (SW3) **Eight Bells** Public gardens
CHELSEA (SW3) **King's Head** Public gardens
CHELSEA (SW3) **Queen's Arms** Garden
CHISWICK (W4) **George IV** Garden
CHISWICK (W4) (Strand-on-the-Green) **Bell & Crown** Riverside patio
CHISWICK (W4) (Strand-on-the-Green) **Bull's Head** Riverside
CHISWICK (W4) (Strand-on-the-Green) **City Barge** Riverside patio
CITY (Fleet St, EC4) **Cheshire Cheese** Children's facilities on back verandah
CITY (Thames St, EC4) **Samuel Pepys** Riverside
CLAPHAM COMMON (SW4, south side) **Old Windmill** All of Clapham Common
COCKFOSTERS **Trent** Garden
EAST BARNET **Prince of Wales** Large garden
EDMONTON (N18) **Cooks Ferry Inn** Play area
ENFIELD **Boundary House** Swings, roundabouts, toys
ENFIELD (River bank) **Crown & Horseshoes** Riverside, play area with climbing frame
GREENFORD **Black Horse** Canalside garden
GREENWICH (SE10) **Cutty Sark** Riverside patio
GREENWICH (SE10) **Gipsy Moth** Riverside verandah
HAMMERSMITH **Blue Anchor** Riverside patio
HAMMERSMITH **Rutland** Riverside patio

MAP 3

HAMPSTEAD (NW3) **Flask** Small garden
HAMPSTEAD HEATH (NW3) **Jack Straw's Castle** Heathside
HAMPSTEAD HEATH (NW3) **Roebuck** Children's garden
HAMPSTEAD HEATH (NW3) **Spaniards** Heathside
HARLESDEN (NW10) **Grand Junction Arms** Canalside garden
HAYES **Brook House** Play garden
ISLEWORTH **London Apprentice** Patio and small garden
KENSINGTON (W10) **Narrow Boat** Canalside
KENSINGTON (Edwardes Square) **Scarsdale Arms** Garden and trees
KINGSTON **Row Barge** Riverside patio, near bridge
LAMBETH (SE1) **Old Father Thames** Riverside
MORTLAKE **Charlie Butler** Patio
MORTLAKE **Ship** Large waterside patio, next to brewery by boat race winning post
OSTERLEY **Hare & Hounds** Garden
OSTERLEY **Osterley Park** Garden
PINNER **George IV** Riverside garden
PUTNEY (SW15) **Duke's Head** Riverside patio
PUTNEY (SW15) **Green Man** Commonside
PUTNEY (SW15) **Star & Garter** Towpath patio
PUTNEY VALE **Robin Hood** Garden
RICHMOND **White Cross** Riverside
ROEHAMPTON (SW15) **Windmill** Commonside
ROTHERHITHE (SE16) **May Flower** Riverside verandah
TEDDINGTON LOCK (Broom Road) **Anglers** Riverside garden
TWICKENHAM **Pope's Grotto** Garden
TWICKENHAM (Embankment) **Queen's Head** Riverside garden
WANDSWORTH (SW18) **Ship** Patio
WAPPING (E1) **Prospect of Whitby** Riverside verandah
WAPPING (E1) **Town of Ramsgate** Riverside
WIMBLEDON **Hand in Hand** Commonside, games room for children

SURREY

BAGSHOT **Foresters Arms** Garden and play area
BEARE GREEN (nr Dorking) **Dukes Head** Swings and play horses in garden
BROCKHAM (nr Betchworth) **Royal Oak** Garden with sandpit and swings
BROOK **Dog & Pheasant** Play area
CAMBERLEY (London Road) **Staff** Garden, play area
CHERTSEY **Cricketers** Riverside garden
CLAYGATE **Folly Arms** Play area in garden, commonside
CRANLEIGH **Leathern Bottle** Garden, play area
EAST MOLESEY **Ferry Boat** Riverside patio
ENGLEFIELD GREEN **Barley Mow** Garden on the green
EWHURST (Pitch Hill) **Windmill** Garden, play area and views
FOREST GREEN **Parrot** Garden and village green
GODALMING (High Street) **Kings Arms & Royal** Aviary, garden
GREAT BOOKHAM **Anchor** Garden, play area
GUILDFORD **Britannia** Riverside garden
GUILDFORD **Farmers** Riverside garden
HAMPTON (Thames Street) **Old Bell** Patio overlooking river
HAMPTON COURT (Toyne Place) **Mitre** Large riverside gardens, moorings
LIGHTWATER **Red Lion** Children's facilities and garden
LINGFIELD **Greyhound** Children's facilities and garden
MERSTHAM **Iron Horse** Children's facilities and garden
MICKLEHAM **William IV** Garden, play area
NEW HAW **White Hart** Canalside garden
NEWDIGATE **Surrey Oaks** Garden, playground with climbing frame
OCKHAM **Hautboy** Garden, play area
PIRBRIGHT **Cricketers** Garden and village green
REDHILL **Lakers** Children's facilities

MAP 3

RIPLEY   Jovial Sailor   Canalside and swings
SALFORDS (nr Redhill)   General Napier   Garden and swings
SEND (Woking Road)   New Inn   Garden and canal
STAINES (Thames Street)   Pack Horse   Small riverside patio with moorings
STAINES (The Hythe)   Swan   Patio, riverside, gardens with moorings
SUNBURY-ON-THAMES   Phoenix   Riverside garden, play area, moorings
THAMES DITTON (Queens Road)   Albany   Lawns overlooking river, own moorings
THORPE (nr Egham)   Rose & Crown   Garden and village green
TILFORD   Barley Mow   Garden and village green
WALTON-ON-THAMES (Manor Road)   Swan   Large lawn, river with moorings and slip
WOKING   Sovereigns   Garden and play area

WEST SUSSEX

AMBERLEY   Sportsmans   Views and play area
ANSTY   Ansty Cross   Garden, swings and see-saw
ARUNDEL   White Swan   Large garden and play area
BILLINGSHURST   Old Six Bells   Large play area
BOGNOR   Martletts   Rocking horse and swings in garden
BRAMBER   Castle   Garden and swings
BUCKS GREEN   Fox   Garden, play area
BURGESS HILL   Potters Arms   Garden, swings, play area
CHILGROVE   White Horse   Garden and village green
CLAYTON   Jack & Jill   Wendy house, swings and sandpit
CRAWLEY   Grasshopper   Garden with swings
CRAWLEY   Swan   Children's facilities and garden
CUCKFIELD   Wheatsheaf   Garden, play area
EASEBOURNE (nr Midhurst)   White Horse   Garden and Wendy house
EAST WITTERING   Royal Oak   Garden, play area
FAYGATE   Cherry Tree   Garden and children's facilities
GORING   Bull   Playground in walled garden
HASSOCKS   Thatched Inn   Garden, play area with swings
HAYLING ISLAND   Ferry Boat   Waterside garden
HORSTED KEYNES   Green Man   Play area
HURSTPIERPOINT   New Inn   Children's facilities in hall
LINDFIELD   Red Lion   Garden with swings and play area
MIDHURST   Spread Eagle   Gardens and lawns
PEASE POTTAGE   Grapes   Garden, play area (at end of Motorway)
PETWORTH   Angel   Garden, play area, facilities
PULBOROUGH   Swan   Terrace and riverside meadows
PULBOROUGH   White Horse   Garden and views
RUSTINGTON   Windmill   Children's playground
SELSEY   Fisherman's Joy   Swings and gardens
SELSEY   Lifeboat   Swings in garden
SHOREHAM   Bridge   Riverside garden
SHOREHAM   Green Jacket   Children's facilities
SHOREHAM   Royal George   Village pond
SOUTHWICK   Romans   Children's facilities
TWO ASH (nr Horsham)   Bax Castle   Garden, play area
WEST CHILTINGTON   Elephant & Castle   Garden, play area
WEST ITCHENOR   Ship   Garden, play area, children's facilities
WISBOROUGH GREEN   Cricketers   On village green
WORTHING   Cricketers   On village green
WORTHING   Half Brick   Overlooking sea
YAPTON   Maypole   Play area and garden

EAST SUSSEX

ALFRISTON   Star   Famous ancient pub with children's facilities

MAP 3

BATTLE **Squirrel Inn** Garden and swings
BATTLE **Wellington** Garden play area
BEACHY HEAD **Beachy Head** Garden, headland, common and cafe
BEXHILL **Wheatsheaf** Garden and swings
BLACKBOYS **Blackboys** Garden, play area and pond
BODIAM **Castle** Castle view, garden and play area
BRIGHTON **Belvedere** On beach, under arches
BRIGHTON **Wellington** Games room
BURWASH **Bell** Children's facilities and garden
CHAILEY **Five Bells** Children's facilities
CHAILEY **Swan** Garden with swings
COWBEACH (nr Hailsham) **Merry Harriers** Garden, play area
CROWBOROUGH **Crow & Gate** Garden, play area
DANEHILL **Coach & Horses** Garden, play area, swings and climbing frame
EAST DEAN **Tiger** Commonside garden
EASTBOURNE **Archery** Seaside and children's facilities
FLETCHING **Cock** Garden, play area
FOREST ROW **Ashdown Forest** Forest play area
GLYNDE **Trevor** Garden with play area
HAILSHAM **Bricklayers Arms** Garden with play area and dovecote
HASTINGS **Cambridge** Children's facilities
HASTINGS **Duke of Wellington** Children's facilities
HOOE (nr Ninfield) **Red Lion** Children's facilities and garden
HOLLINGTON **Hollington** Children's facilities and garden
HOVE **Sussex** Village pond
HOVE **Sussex Cricketers** County cricket ground, play area
NEWHAVEN **Ark** Quayside patio
NEWMARKET (nr Lewes) **Newmarket** Garden, play area, Wendy house
PEACEHAVEN **Peacehaven** Children's play area and facilities overlooking sea
PLUMPTON **Gun** Garden, swings, play area
RYE **Rumples** Children's facilities and garden
RYE HARBOUR **William the Conqueror** Quayside
SEAFORD **Old Plough** Children's facilities
SCAYNES HILL **Farmers** Garden and village green
SEDLESCOMBE (nr Battle) **Queens Head** Garden with aviary and animals
SIDLEY (nr Bexhill) **New Inn** Commonside and children's facilities
UDIMORE **Kings Head** Garden, occasional festivals and children's facilities
WINCHELSEA BEACH **Ship** Garden, play area
WITHERENDEN HILL (Burwash) **Kicking Donkey** Children's facilities and hop fields

KENT

ALL HALLOWS (nr Bexley) **British Pilot** Children's facilities and garden
ASHFORD **Golden Ball** Garden, play area and bat and trap
BELVEDERE **Old Leather Bottle** Views over Thames estuary
BEXLEY **Three Blackbirds** Play area with swings
BIRLING (nr West Malling) **Nevill Bull** Children's facilities
BISHOPSBOURNE **Mermaid** Children's facilities
BROADSTAIRS **Barnaby Rudge** Children's facilities
BROOKLAND **Woolpack** Children's facilities and garden
BROOMFIELD (nr Herne Bay) **Huntsman & Horn** Children's facilities
BURHAM **Royal Albert** Children's facilities and garden
CHATHAM **Ordinary Fellow** Children's facilities
CHELSFIELD (Well Hill) **Kent Hounds** Isolated garden, children's facilities
CHILLENDEN **Griffins Head** Garden and games room
CONYER **Ship** Waterside garden
DARTFORD **Plough** Children's facilities
DYMCHURCH **City of London** Children's facilities
EAST FARLEIGH (nr Maidstone) **Horseshoe** Children's facilities
EAST PECKHAM **Man of Kent** Riverside garden

MAP 3

EASTCHURCH (nr Sheerness) **Wheatsheaf** Children's facilities
EWELL MINNIS **Newcastle** Garden play area
FOLKESTONE **Clarendon** Children's facilities
FORDWICH **Fordwich Arms** Riverside gardens
HERSDEN (nr Canterbury) **Shrew Beshrew'd** Children's facilities
HYTHE **Botolphs Bridge** Canalside
IGHTHAM COMMON (nr Sevenoaks) **Harrow** Children's facilities and garden
KESTON **Greyhound** Commonside garden
KILNDOWN **Globe & Rainbow** Children's facilities and garden
KINGSDOWN **Zetland Arms** Waterside garden
LEYSDOWN (nr Sheerness) **Rose & Crown** Children's facilities
LITTLEBOURNE **Evenhill** Children's facilities and garden
LOOSE (nr Maidstone) **Star** Children's facilities
LOWER HARDRES **Three Horseshoes** Children's facilities and garden
LUDDESDOWN (nr Rochester) **Cock** Play area in 6 acres
MARGATE **Princess of Wales** Children's facilities
MATFIELD **Star** Children's facilities and garden
NEWNHAM **George** Children's facilities and garden
OARE **Three Mariners** Children's facilities and garden, caravan park
ORPINGTON **Bull** Swings and play area
RAINHAM **Army & Navy** Children's facilities
ROCHESTER **Greyhound** Garden with pets
ST NICHOLAS-AT-WADE **Bell** Games room and garden
SANDWICH **George & Dragon** Children's facilities
SANDWICH **Red Cow** Children's facilities and garden
SEASALTER (nr Whitstable) **Blue Anchor** Children's facilities
SEVENOAKS (London Road) **Dorset Arms** Children's facilities
SHEERNESS **Blacksmiths Arms** Children's facilities
SHIPBOURNE **Chaser** Garden on the village green
SITTINGBOURNE **Foresters Arms** Children's facilities
STANSTED **Black Horse** Garden and children's facilities
STROOD **Bulls Head** Children's facilities
STURRY (Calcot Hill) **Punch** Children's facilities and garden
STURRY (nr Canterbury) **Swan** Children's facilities
SWANLEY **Alma** Garden and swings (near start of M2)
TONBRIDGE **Pinnacles** Play area with swings
UPCHURCH **Brown Jug** Children's facilities
WHITSTABLE **Golden Lion** Children's facilities and garden
WHITSTABLE **Old Neptune** Seashore
WOODCHURCH **Bonny Cravat** Garden and play area

MAP 4

DYFED (see also Map 7)

1 NEW HEDGES   Hunter's Moon
** (Tenby 2630)
Free House. Old pub in own grounds, greatly modernized. Restaurant, bar meals, all times. Gardens with swings and attractive zoo. Children's room upstairs with amusements.
Just off A478 in village centre.

2 KILGETTY Carmarthen Road   Kilgetty
(Saundersfoot 813219)
Felin Foel. Old Victorian village pub with character landlord. Snacks. Family room in back yard with TV and piano. Traditional beer.
On A478.

3 KILGETTY Carmarthen Road
White Horse (Saundersfoot 812818)
Felin Foel. One-time blacksmith's shop. Light meals (except Sun). Snacks. Patio. Small children's snug off main bar (provided they stay there). Traditional ale.
On A478.

4 WHITLAND   Fisher's Arms (W 371)
Felin Foel. Coaching-change house. B & B. Bar meals (closed Sun, 6-day licence). Garden, off which is a religious meeting-room of yesteryear now used as family room, leading to bar. Traditional beer.
On A40, on bend, east end of town.

5 ST DOGMAELS (Poppit Sands)   Webley
** (Cardigan 2085)
Free House. One-time fishermen's pub grown to a small hotel. B & B, restaurant, bar meals. Garden and views. Small children's room off main bar. Bar closed all day Sun. Traditional beer.
On estuary overlooking Cardigan Bay.

6 CARDIGAN Pendre   Commercial
(C 2574)
Felin Foel. Old coaching house. Car park near. B & B, light snacks. Family/children's area in back yard and family room off main passage. Traditional beer. Market Mon and Sat all day. (Bar closed Sun.)
In town centre.

7 LAMPETER   Railway (L 422439)
Free House. Victorian pub. Snacks. Patio, porch verandah used as family room off car park. Traditional beer.
On edge of town by railway.

8 ABERYSTWYTH Market   Angel
(A 617878)
Bass. Small old character pub. Roadside parking, restricted. Bar snacks. Small family room off passage. Traditional beer.
Off A481 in town centre in one-way street.

9 GOGINAN   Druids (Capel Bangor 650)
Free House. One-time lead-mining pub. Light snacks. Large family room off main bar. Traditional beer. (6-day licence, closed on Sun.)
On A44 in village centre.

10 BYNEA   Lewis Arms (Llanelli 2878)
Felin Foel. Victorian steel-box pub. Bar lunches Mon-Fri. Snacks all times. Garden, swings, shutes, Dining room used as family room. Traditional beer.
On A484 overlooking Penclawdd Hills.

WEST GLAMORGAN

11 LLANRHIDIAN   North Gower
** (Reynoldston 242)
Free House. Mock Tudor between-wars private house recently converted. Restaurant evenings except Sun when T d'hôte lunch. Bar meals. Large garden with lawns. Family room off main entrance.
On B4271 at junction with B4295.

12 MORRISTON   Red Lion
(Swansea 73206)
Bass. Main-road large pub. Bar meals. Snacks other times. Two gardens. Children's room (Mon, Thurs only) off lounge bar and garden. Traditional beer.
On A48 ½m from J45 M4.

13 GARNANT   Lamb & Flag
Buckleys. Old-fashioned, small, miner's pub. Draw in. Two small rooms either side of entrance for families up to 8 pm. Traditional beer.
On A474, Neath end of village.

MID GLAMORGAN

14 PORTHCAWL   New Brodgen (P 3727)
Whitbread. Brick town pub, built early this century. Snacks all times. Patio yard at back with large barn for families. Own children's bar at weekends and summer with amusements.
On A4106 on east side.

MAP 4

GWENT

15 RHIWDERIN Caerphilly Road Rhiwderin (R 3234)
Bass. Victorian brick pub. Light bar lunches (not Sun). Snacks evenings. Family verandah off car park to lounge bar. Traditional beer.
On A478 1½m N of J28 M4.

16 CALDICOT Good Measure (C 420266)
Whitbread. Typical small-town pub. Bar meals. Playing field and bowling green at back. Children, if supervised, may use skittle alley in inclement weather up to 8 pm.
Off B4245 Chepstow/Newport road in village centre.

17 CLYTHA Clytha Arms (Gobien 206)
Free House. Private house converted. B & B. Restaurant (not Tues). Bar meals all times. Garden and lawns, family room off lounge bar.
On A40 3m W of Raglan.

18 LLANTHONY Abbey (Crucorney 487)

Free House. 15th C priory converted. B & B. Restaurant (evenings) Bar meals. Large garden. Children may use the cloisters (no tables or seats). Traditional beer.
Off B4423 3m W of A465.

POWYS

19 BRECON Gremlin (B 3829)
Free House. 17th C pub greatly changed. Roadside parking restricted. B & B. Restaurant, bar meals. Garden. Passage way from bar to garden used for children. Traditional beer.
On A40 Abergavenny side of town.

20 LLANDRINDOD WELLS Llanerch (LW 2086)
Free House. 17th C coaching house. Accommodation. Restaurant, bar meals. Large garden, play area, with orchard. Family room off main entrance or lounge bar.
In town centre near railway station.

MAP 4
Other pubs to try

DYFED (see also Map 7)

ABERAERON Harbour Master Garden overlooking harbour
ABERYSTWYTH Plough Children's facilities and garden
AMROTH (nr Narberth) New Inn Lawns and caravan
CARDIGAN Eagle Riverside garden
HAVERFORDWEST County Children's facilities and garden
HAVERFORDWEST Bristol Trader Riverside garden
LITTLE HAVEN Swan Quayside patio
PEMBROKE Ferry Waterside

WEST GLAMORGAN

BISHOPSTON Plough & Harrow Children's facilities and garden
GOWERTON Welcome to Gower Play area
LLANRHIDIAN Dolphin Swings
THE MUMBLES (Bishops Town) Pilot Waterside
PORT TALBOT (Margam Road) Twelve Knights Children's facilities and garden (nr J39 M4)

MID GLAMORGAN

KENFIG Prince of Wales Children's facilities and seaside garden
PORTHCAWL High Tide Waterside
PORTHCAWL Jolly Sailor On the green, with garden

SOUTH GLAMORGAN

MAP 4

CARDIFF   Red House   Waterside garden
DINAS POWIS   Cross Keys   Village green
MOULTON (nr Barry)   Three Horseshoes   Gardens, swings, donkey

GWENT

CAERLEON   Hanbury Arms   Riverside garden
CHEPSTOW   George   Garden, play area
LLANFIHANGEL CRUCORNEY   Skirrid   Mountain, nice garden, Wales oldest pub
MONMOUTH   Beaufort Arms   Children's facilities and garden
PONTYPOOL   Goytre Arms   Garden, swings
SEBASTOPOL (nr Pontypool)   Open Hearth   Canalside garden
WENTLOOGE   Church House Inn   Garden with swings and amenities

POWYS

CRICKHOWELL   Bridgend   Waterside, River Usk
GILWERN   Navigation   Garden to canal
LLANDRINDOD WELLS   Metropole   Children's facilities, play area
LLANGYNIDR   Coach & Horses   Canalside garden
LLECHRYD   Carpenter's Arms   Play area
TRETOWER   Nant-y-Flin Cider Mill   Lawns, orchard, cider mill

MAP 5

GLOUCESTERSHIRE (see also Map 2)

1 COLEFORD Berryhill Pike   Pike House
(C 3010)
Whitbread. The old toll house rebuilt in 1923. Bar snacks. Garden with swings. Skittle room off public bar used as family room, daytimes and early evening. Traditional beer.
On A4136 in Forest of Dean.

2 COLEFORD Hillersland   Rock
(Dean 32367)
Free House. One-time private house with fine views. Snacks all times. Large garden with swings. Family room off garden, in old skittle alley.
On Symonds Yat road, 1m N off A4136 in Forest of Dean.

3 FRAMILODE PASSAGE   Darell Arms
(Gloucester 740320)
Whitbread. Private house converted. Substantial bar meals. Large garden, play area, swings. Family room off main entrance on right. Traditional ale.
W 3m off A38, signed Framilode Passage. 3m J13 M5.

4 UPPER FRAMILODE   Ship
(Framilode 260)
Whitbread. Small bargees' pub, modernized. Bar meals. Canalside garden. Family room off main bar into garden.
W off A38 on B4071 in village centre. 2m J13 M5.

5 BEECHPIKE (nr Elkstone)   Highwayman
(Miserden 221)
Arkells. One-time farm cottage of Cotswold stone. Restaurant, bar meals. Garden. Family room off garden or main bar. Traditional beer.
On A417 N of Cirencester.

6 COLESBOURNE   Colesbourne
(Coberley 376)
Wadworths. One-time coaching house. Buffet, hot special and steaks. Bar meals. Garden with amusements. Families welcome in buffet room whether eating or not. Traditional beer.
On A435 N of Cirencester.

7 CHEDWORTH Queen Street
Seven Tuns (Fosse Bridge 242)
Courage. Character Cotswold stone pub, once a brewery. Snacks. Patio. Children's room with TV through main bar. Traditional beer.
Off the beaten track in village centre, S of Cheltenham.

8 BIBURY   Catherine Wheel (B 250)
Courage. 17th C Cotswold stone. Lunches daily, snacks in evening. Garden. Children's room a conservatory off the garden. Traditional beer.
On A433 on edge of village, NE of Cirencester.

9 STOW-ON-THE-WOLD   Bell
Whitbread. Cotswold stone, creeper covered. B & B, bar snacks. Garden with fine views. Family room off main entrance.
On A436 on south edge of town.

10 CHIPPING CAMPDEN High Street
Lygon Arms (Evesham 840318)
Free House. One of England's famous old coaching houses in Cotswold stone. Unrestricted roadside parking. B & B. Bar meals all times. Coaching yard with seats. Family room (the breakfast room) off main entrance. Traditional beer.
In town centre.

OXFORDSHIRE (see also Map 2)

11 EPWELL (nr Banbury)   Chandler's Arms
(Swalcliffe 344)
Hook Norton. 17th C stone pub off the beaten track. Bar snacks. Garden. Family room off garden or small main bar. Traditional beer.
N off B4036 W of Banbury.

12 LITTLE BOURTON   Plough
(Cropredy 222)
Bass. One-time smallholding on main road. Bar snacks. Small patio. Children's room off lounge with games and TV.
On A423 N of Banbury 2m.

13 ADDERBURY (nr Banbury) High St   Bell
(Banbury 810338)
Free House. Cottages converted in country village. Roadside parking. Bar snacks. Garden. Family room off passage to main bar. Traditional beer.
On A423 2m S of Banbury.

14 AYNHO (nr Banbury)   Great Western
(Goddington 38288)
Hook Norton. Canalside bargees' pub, one-time railway hotel. Bar meals, except Mon. Garden with frame. Family room off main entrance. Traditional beer.
E off A41 on B4031 S of Banbury.

MAP 5

15 WOOTTON High Street   King's Head
(Woodstock 811346)
Bass. Once 17th C cottages in Cotswold
stone. Near Blenheim Palace. Roadside
parking. Snacks. Garden with aviary and
Aunt Sally. Children may use hall
between bars and garden. Traditional
beer.
On A34 1½m W of Woodstock.

16 WITNEY Newland Oxford Road   Griffin
(W 2419)
Wadworths. Typical country-town local.
Snacks. Patio. Yard with Aunt Sally.
Family room with TV. Traditional beer.
1m from town centre, just off A40.

NORTHAMPTONSHIRE (see also Map 6)

17 COSGROVE   Navigation
** (Ardley Govion 542105)
Watneys. Old bargees' house on Grand
Union Canal. Snacks. Garden on waterside. Large children's room with games
and own 'bridge'. Verandah overlooking
canal.
1m E off A508, N of Wolverton.

18 WESTON   Crown (Sulgrave 328)
Free House. One-time farmhouse. B & B.
Home-cooked full meals (limited on Sun).
Garden. Family room with piano off the
main bar. Traditional ale.
E off B4525 between Banbury and
Towcester.

19 FARTHINGSTONE   King's Arms
(Preston Capes 604)
Free House. Rebuilt in stone on old
church house site. Full meals daily. Garden at back off car park. Family room
through main bar. Traditional beer.
3m off A5 S of Weedon.

20 WEEDON BECK   Narrow Boat
(W 40536)
* Charles Wells. Old bargees' pub
overlooking canal. Meals 7 days a week.
Cheese skittles. Garden with peacocks
and aviary. Large family room off car
park. Traditional ale.
On A5 Watling Street, 3m from J16 M1.

21 WELFORD   Swan (W 481)
Marstons. Small coaching change house.
Hot snacks (and meals if prepared to
wait for preparation). Garden. Cheese-
skittles alley used as family room. Traditional beer.
On A50 at N end of village. Near county

border and Sulby reservoir.

22 CLAY COTON (nr Crick)   Fox & Hounds
** (Swinford 363)
Free House. One-time farm cottage.
Snacks. Cheese skittles. Garden. Children's room with games off the car park
and main bar.
3m from motorway J18. N in Crick. Hard
to find.

WARWICKSHIRE & WEST MIDLANDS

23 HILLMORTON (nr Rugby)
Old Royal Oak (Rugby 61401)
Free House. Old bargees' canalside pub
on Oxon canal. Full meals all times. Garden alongside canal. Small family room
off car park. Traditional beer (only Thurs
to Sun in cellar bar).
On A428 W of J18 M1.

24 KINGSBURY   Royal Oak
(Tamworth 872339)
Marstons. Victorian red-brick village
local. Bar snacks. Garden. Family room
off passage in main entrance. Traditional
beer.
W off A51 in village, NE of Birmingham.

25 WALSALL Wallows Lane
King George V (W 26130)
Bass. large pub built 1937. Snacks,
limited evenings. Large garden. Family
room at the back off the garden. Traditional beer.
Off A461, off J9 M6 by Walsall football
ground.

26 WEDNESFIELD Amos Lane   Red Lion
(Wolverhampton 732842)
Bass. Between-wars, large crossroads
pub. Lunches Mon-Fri. Snacks all times.
Large garden at back. Family/children's
room through off-sales, off car park.
Traditional ale.
In housing area ½m off A462, 3¾m W of
J10 M6.

27 WILLENHALL (nr Wolverhampton)
Stafford Street   Tiger (W 65356)
Simpkiss. 3-storey Victorian pub. Restricted parking. Snacks. Yard at back
with family room off it. Traditional beer.
2½m from J10 M6. In town centre on
one-way system.

28 DARLASTON Cemetery Road   Railway
(Birmingham 5262604)
Bass. Victorian pub of character. Road-

MAP 5

side parking. Snacks lunchtime. Waste land in front, children's room at back at end of passage. Traditional ale. On A4038 ½m from J10 M6.

29 BRIERLEY HILL Delph Road Vine
(BH 78293)
Bathams. Quaint Victorian pub known locally as Bull and Bladder. Cold table, lunches (not Sun). Patio with rabbits, etc. Children's room off passage at back. Traditional ale.
Off A4100, alongside Bathams Delph Brewery.

30 BRIERLEY HILL Brettell Lane
Foley Arms
Simpkiss. Small Victorian pub, 'the tap'. Snacks. Small family room off main entrance, with pool table. Traditional beer. On A461, alongside Simpkiss Brewery.

EREFORD & WORCESTER

31 FOWNHOPE Forge & Ferry (F 391)
Free House. Quaint cider house of yesteryear. Basket meals. Garden. Large entrance foyer used as family room off main bar. Traditional beer.
Just off B4224 in village centre, down lane to River Wye.

32 ROSS-ON-WYE Broad Street
King Charles II (RoW 2039)
Free House. One-time coaching house and tavern. Restricted roadside parking. Restaurant (not always winter). Bar meals. Children's room off main entrance. Traditional beer.
In town centre. Off A40.

33 WALFORD Spread Eagle
(Ross-on-Wye 2891)
Whitbread. Once Victorian farm/pub. B & B, bar meals. Garden with amusements. Skittle alley with pool table used as family room.
On B4228 in village centre, S of Ross.

34 SYMOND'S YAT WEST Old Ferrie Inn
(SY 890232)
Free House. 15th C ferry house with charter. B & B. Restaurant, bar meals. Riverside patio. Children's room off main bar overlooking river. Traditional ale.
1m off A40 in west part of village. NE of Monmouth.

35 PETERCHURCH King's Head (P 271)
Free House. Was farm smallholding.

Snacks. Garden with ponies in paddock. Families use large pool room off the car park.
Off B4348 in Golden Valley. SE of Hay-on-Wye.

36 DORSTONE Pandy (Peterchurch 273)
Free House. Small 17th C leather works (Welsh name). B & B, bar meals. Garden with amusements. New children's room off garden. Traditional beer.
¼m off B4348 in best-kept village centre. SE of Hay-on-Wye.

37 HARDWICK Royal Oak (Clifford 248)
Free House. Old farm cottage converted. B & B. Bar snacks. Garden and lawn. Small family room off main passage.
On B4348, isolated. E of Hay-on-Wye.

38 BRIMFIELD Roebuck (B 230)
Allied. Greatly enlarged 17th C village pub. Bar meals. Large garden. Family room off car park in separate building. Traditional beer.
On A49 S of Ludlow.

39 TENBURY WELLS Teme Street Ship
(TW 810269)
Ansells. 17th C coaching house. Lunchtime substantial snacks. Patio. Family room off patio in back yard. Traditional beer.
In quaint village centre, ¼m off A456. SE of Ludlow.

40 NEWNHAM BRIDGE Tavern (NB 331)
Free House. Victorian railway pub before Beeching's axe fell. Basket meals, evenings only. Patio and orchard play area. Children may use pool room off main bar. Traditional beer.
Just off A456, overlooking it, SW of Bewdley.

41 LINDRIDGE Nag's Head
* (Eardiston 234)
Marsdons. Isolated, attractive old farmers' cottage, amongst orchards and hop gardens. Snacks. Garden with small hut for children's room. Traditional beer.
On A43 6m E of Tenbury Wells.

42 CALLOW HILL (nr Bewdley)
Royal Forester (Rock 266286)
Bass. Old forest cottage, one-time cider house. Sandwiches all times. Garden and orchard. Family room opposite main bar. Traditional ale.
On A456 3m W of Bewdley.

MAP 5

SHROPSHIRE

43 CLEOBURY MORTIMER   Talbot
(CM 205)
Free House. Black and white house said to date from 1560. B & B. Restaurant, bar lunches. Family room off lounge bar. On A4117, 4m W of Bewdley.

44 BISHOPS CASTLE   Three Tuns (BC 229)
* Free House. 17th C home brew pub, one of the four left in the country. Home cooking special lunch, salads summer. Snacks other times. Garden with menagerie and patio in brew yard. Family room on verandah overlooking brewery. Own traditional beer.
On B4385. Almost in Wales.

45 WENTNOR   Crown (Linley 613)
* Free House. Small 17th C village pub on the Long Mynd hills. Bar meals (not Sun eve). Patio and field with children's/ family room in brew house, off patio. Traditional beer.
2½m N off A489 Bishops Castle road. N of Craven Arms.

46 BRIDGNORTH Hospital Street   Fox
(B 3318)
Allied. 18th C corner house near river. Bar meals except Sun mornings. Patio garden with swings at back. Children's room off lounge entrance with amusements. Traditional beer.
On A442, S end of town.

47 OAKENGATES The Nob   Bird in Hand
(Telford 613922)
Banks. Modern red-brick pub. Rolls on Saturday. Woodlands to play. Small children's room off main entrance hall off car park. Traditional beer.
½m off B54069 in woods on part-private road through new estate.

48 LONGDON-UPON-TERN   Tayleur Arms
(High Ercall 335)
Davenports. Typical large Victorian country pub. Steak bar (not Sun lunch and Mon eve). Bar meals. Garden. Front verandah for families, and if eating, the steak bar. Traditional beer.
On B5163 N of Telford.

49 ELLESMERE   Railway (E 2254)
Greenall Whitley. Victorian 3-storey building. Restricted daytime parking. Snacks all times. Patio at back with racing pigeons, children's/family room off it. In market square in town centre, SW of Whitchurch.

STAFFORDSHIRE (see also Map 8)

50 WIMBLEBURY   Lamb & Flag
(Heath Hayes 77314)
Allied. Typical Victorian mining pub. Wild area and children's room off main entrance passage. Traditional ale.
Just off B5190 at Heath Hayes roundabout, 1m N.

51 GREAT HAYWOOD   Clifford Arms
(Little Haywood 881321)
Bass. Victorian coaching house. Bar lunches, buffet weekends. Garden with swings. Children's room off garden; near canal and stately house. Traditional beer. ½m off A51 in village centre. E of Stafford.

52 STRETTON (nr Burton) Derby Road Beech (Burton 61811)
Marstons. Mock Tudor between-wars main-road pub. Bar snacks. Large garden with numerous amusements. Old dining room (off the garden) used as family room until 8 pm.
On A38, on E outskirts of famous brewing centre.

DERBYSHIRE

53 EGGINTON   Every Arms
(Burton 703284)
Bass. Old bargees' pub backing on to canal. Snacks all times. Large garden. Jubilee swingboats and other amusements. Family room off main passage with juke box and pin table.
On A38 dual carriageway, NE of Burton-on-Trent.

LEICESTERSHIRE

54 SHEEPY MAGNA   Black Horse
(Tamworth 880555)
Marstons. 17th C popular village pub. Lunches Mon-Fri. Patio with small alcove used as family room between bar and car park.
On B4116, E of Tamworth.

55 PINWALL (nr Atherstone)   Red Lion
(Atherstone 2223)
Bass. One-time farmhouse. Garden and use of lounge as family room. Traditional beer.

MAP 5

On B4116 just off B5000 in small hamlet, E of Tamworth.

56 NORTON-JUXTA-TWYCROSS
* **Moores Arms** (Tamworth 880364)
Marstons. Old farm cottages. Snacks. Garden with badminton. Back stables as family room with table tennis. Traditional beer.
East off A444 opposite zoo at Twycross. N of Nuneaton.

57 HEATHER   Crown (Ibstock 60367)
Free House. One-time posting house. Snacks. Garden with swings. Large games room at back through bar or from garden. Traditional beer.
On B591 in village centre SW of Coalville.

58 WHITWICK   Forest Rock
(Coalville 31495)
Allied. Old quarrymen's house (quarry nearby still working). Meals all times. Garden. Children's room off passage with games. Traditional beer.
On B587, out of town at crossroads.

59 COPT OAK   Copt Oak (Markfield 2353)
* Marstons. One-time coaching stage. Basket lunches (except Sun). Rolls other times. Garden at back and large family room with TV off car park entrance.
East off B591, 2m from J22 M1.

60 CROPSTON   Bradgate Arms
(Anstey 2120)
Free House. Old village pub, brewed own beer. Snacks. Garden at back with family room off the car park. Traditional beer.
In village centre on A5328 near reservoir. NW of Leicester.

61 QUORN (Quorndon) Meeting Street
Blacksmith's Arms (Q 42751)
Marstons. Typical, small, unspoilt village pub. Snacks. Patio seats in car park. Family room off lounge bar and car park. Traditional beer.
Off A6 at bridge in the village.

62 BARROW-ON-SOAR Mill Lane
* **Navigation** (Quorn 42842)
Shipstone. One time bargees' house. Roadside parking. Snacks lunchtime. Large garden by canal. Family room off main entrance. Traditional beer.
Off A5238 on canal. SE of Loughborough.

63 LONG CLAWSON   Crown & Plough
(Melton Mowbray 822124)
Home Brewery. 18th C rambling coaching inn. Bar snacks. Garden. Several rooms, one the games room, can be used by families. Traditional beer.
N off A606 2½m NE of Melton Mowbray.

64 SYSTON   Gate Hangs Well
** (Leicester 805850)
Free House. Red-brick house on site of old coaching house. Meals winter, snacks. Large garden with swings and back verandah as children's room. Traditional beer.
On A46 (Newark side) N of Leicester.

65 SYSTON   Queen Victoria
(Leicester 605750)
Everards. Typical small-town Victorian pub. Snacks. Patio in courtyard off which is a large family room.
On A46 N of Leicester.

66 LEICESTER Asquith Boulevard
Aberdale (L 882231)
Everards. Modern estate pub. Light snacks. Large family room off car park. Traditional beer available in one bar if asked for.
Off main Northampton Road A50.

67 BARWELL Chapel Street   Cross Keys
(Earl Shilton 43535)
Bass. 18th C town pub. Bar snacks. Garden with swings. Covered courtyard used as family room and games room, through main bar. Traditional beer.
In town centre, N of Hinckley.

68 FROLESWORTH   Plough & Harrow
(Leire 209347)
Bass. Typical village pub. Lunches Mon-Fri. Light snacks other times. Small garden. Back verandah closed in as children's room. Traditional beer.
Off beaten track, SE of Hinckley, NE of A5.

69 ULLESTHORPE   Chequers
(Leire 209214) `
Davenports. Old 18th C cottages in village. Accommodation. Restaurant (not Sat, Mon or all day Sun). Bar snacks. Patio. Children's room in alcove bar and restaurant. Traditional ale.
Off B577 SE of Nuneaton.

70 WALCOTE   Black Horse
(Lutterworth 2684)
Free House. Old coaching stage. Limited

MAP 5

home-made bar meals. Patio. Upstairs pool room used as family room. Traditional beer.
On A427 1m E from J20 M1.

71 HUSBANDS BOSWORTH   Cherry Tree

(Market Harborough 880369) Watneys. Rebuilt brick house. Meals. Garden. Children's room off garden at back. Traditional beer.
On A427 in village centre. W of Market Harborough.

MAP 5
Other pubs to try

GLOUCESTERSHIRE (see also Map 2)

ASHLEWORTH   Boat   Garden overlooking Severn
BOURTON-ON-THE-WATER   Old New Inn   Model village in garden
CINDERFORD   Woodlands   Children's facilities
CRANHAM (nr Gloucester)   Royal William   Children's facilities
NEWENT   King's Arms   Children's facilities
NORTH CERNEY (nr Cirencester)   Buthurst Arms   Riverside garden
PAINSWICK (nr Stroud)   Falcon   Bowling green
PURTON WEST (Old Severn Bridge)   Berkeley Hunt   Children's facilities and garden
SHEEPSCOMBE   Butcher's Arms   Garden with views
SLIMBRIDGE   Tudor Arms   Canalside garden
TEWKESBURY   Black Bear Inn   Riverside garden
TIRLEY   Haw Bridge   Children's facilities

OXFORDSHIRE (see also Map 2)

HETHE   Whitmore Arms   Garden and play area
HOOK NORTON   Sun Inn   Garden and animals
KIDLINGTON (nr Oxford)   Black Horse   Swings
KIDLINGTON (nr Oxford)   Wise Alderman   Riverside
MIDDLE BARTON   Carpenter's Arms   Riverside and gardens
MURCOTT   Nut Tree   Village green and pond
NORTH KINGSEY   Fishes   Large garden
OXFORD   Head of the River   Riverside terrace
OXFORD   Isis   Riverside
POUNDON (nr Bicester)   Sow & Pigs   Garden with swings, pond with ducks
SOUTH LEIGH   Mason's Arms   Peacocks and lawns
SWINBROOK (Burford)   Swan   Riverside
WOOTTON (nr Wantage)   Killingworth Castle   Swings and frame

BUCKINGHAMSHIRE (see also Maps 3 & 6)

GREAT LINFORD (nr Newport Pagnell)   Black Horse   Canalside
OLD WOLVERTON   Galleon   Canalside garden
OVING (Aylesbury)   Black Boy   Panoramic views with play area
WENDOVER   Shoulder of Mutton   Aviary
WESTON TURVILLE   Five Bells   Garden, aviary, peacocks
WORMINGHALL   Clivden Arms   Garden and play area

NORTHAMPTONSHIRE (see also Map 6)

DEANSHANGER (Wolverton)   Fox & Hounds   Children's facilities, garden and village gre
EVENLEY   Red Lion   Garden and village green
KETTERING   Prince of Wales   Children's facilities
LITTLE HARROWDEN (Wellingborough)   Ten O'Clock   Play area
LONG BUCKBY (Daventry)   New Inn   Canalside garden

MAP 5

SHUTLANGER **Plough** Garden and animals
STOKE BRUERNE **Boat** Canalside garden

WARWICKSHIRE

ARROW (nr Alcester) **Arrow Mill** Waterside
BASCOTE HEATH (nr Southam) **Fox & Hen** Playground, amusements, soft drinks
BIDFORD-ON-AVON **Pleasure Boat** Riverside garden
COVENTRY **Styvechale Arms** Large play area
COVENTRY **Wallace** Play area
FENNY COMPTON **George & Dragon** Canalside, aviary, camping
GREAT ALNE (nr Alcester) **Mother Huff Cap** Play area, agricultural implements, old cars and cartwheels
HATTON (Warwick) **New Inn** Canalside garden
HOCKLEY HEATH (Solihull) **Reservoir** Garden play area on reservoir
HUNNINGHAM (nr Leamington Spa) **Red Lion** Riverside
MAPPLEBOROUGH GREEN (nr Studeley) **Dog** Playground at back
NAPTON-ON-THE-HILL **Napton Bridge** Canalside
RUGBY **Boat** Canalside garden
STOCKTON (Southam, nr Rugby) **Blue Lias** Canalside and donkey
STRATFORD-ON-AVON **Encore** Riverside
STRATFORD-ON-AVON **Shakespeare** Children's facilities and garden
STRATFORD-ON-AVON **Windmill Inn** Play area
WARWICK (Westgate Street) **Westgate Arms** Racecourse at bottom of garden
WELFORD-ON-AVON **Bell** Village green
WESTON-UNDER-WETHERLEY **Bull** Play area
WOOTTON WAWEN (nr Solihull) **Old Bull's Head** Lawns

WEST MIDLANDS

ACOCKS GREEN (Birmingham) **Dolphin** Bowling green
BLOXWICH (Walsall) **Knave of Hearts** Playground
BRIERLEY HILL (Birmingham) **Plough** Children's facilities
BRIERLEY HILL (Birmingham) **Wall Heath Inn** Playground
KINGS NORTON (Birmingham) **Bull's Head** Village green
KINGSWINFORD **Old Bush** Play area, canal, moorings
KINGSWINFORD **Old Court House** Village green
KINGSWINFORD (Greensforge) **Navigation** Canalside patio
NORTHFIELD (Birmingham) **Old Mill** Playground
PELSALL **Old Bush** Garden and common
SEDGLEY **Jolly Crispin** Children's facilities
SHIRLEY (Solihull) **Drawbridge** Canalside garden
SMALL HEATH (Birmingham) **Horse & Jockey** Children's facilities and garden
SUTTON COLDFIELD **Boat** Canalside
WALSALL **Barley Mow** Canalside garden

HEREFORD & WORCESTERSHIRE

AYMESTREY **Crown** Riverside
BECKFORD **Beckford** Children's facilities and lawns
CAREY **Cottage of Comfort** Garden and play area
CHADDESLEY CORBETT **Swan** Bowling green
CUTNALL GREEN (nr Droitwich) **Old Chequers** Lawns
DROITWICH **Chateau Impney** Own grounds and unusual animals
EVESHAM (Abbey Road) **Vauxhall** Play area
HARTLEBURY **White Hart** Lawns
HEREFORD **Graftonbury** Garden with putting green
HEREFORD **Green Dragon** Children's facilities

MAP 5

HOLT HEATH   **Red Lion**   Children's facilities and garden
MARTIN HUSSINGTREE   **Swan**   Lawns with swings and slide
REDDITCH   **White Hart**   Bowling green
STAUNTON-ON-WYE   **Portway**   Camping and play area
STOKE WORKS   **Boat & Railway**   Canalside (sometimes children's facilities)
STOKE WORKS   **Bowling Green**   Garden and bowling green
STORRIDGE   **New Inn**   Play area and camping
STOURPORT-ON-SEVERN   **Hampstall**   Garden on River Severn
STRETTON SUGWAS (nr Hereford)   **Priory**   Garden and lawns
TIBBERTON   **Bridge**   Canalside garden
UPTON-ON-SEVERN   **Plough**   Riverside garden
WORCESTER   **Star**   Children's facilities, garden and skittle alley

SHROPSHIRE

ATCHAM BRIDGE   **Mytton & Mermaid**   Riverside lawns
DONNINGTON   **White House**   Lawns and play area
DUDDLESTON HEATH   **Fox**   Lawns
IRON BRIDGE   **Bird in Hand**   Riverside garden
IRON BRIDGE   **Swan**   Riverside garden
JACKFIELD (Iron Bridge)   **Half Moon**   Riverside garden
LEINTWARDINE (nr Craven Arms)   **Lion**   Riverside
MADELEY   **All Nations**   Garden (an original home-brew house)
MAESBURY MARSH   **Navigation**   Canalside garden
MILSON (nr Tenbury Wells)   **Trapnell**   Bowling green and swings
PIPEGATE (Market Drayton)   **Chetwood Arms**   Play area
SHREWSBURY   **Boat House**   Riverside
SHREWSBURY   **Corracle**   Lawns and play area
TREFONEN   **Efel**   Country pub, lawns

STAFFORDSHIRE (see also Map 8)

ALREWAS (nr Burton-on-Trent)   **Swan**   Canalside
ASHLEY (nr Market Drayton)   **Robin Hood**   Garden with birds
BRANSTON   **Brewood**   Canalside garden
HIGH OFFLEY   **Anchor**   Garden and canal
PENKRIDGE   **Cross Keys**   Canalside garden
SALT (nr Stafford)   **Holly Bush**   Play area
SEIGHFORD (nr Stafford)   **Seighford**   Own grounds (nr J14 M6)
SHEBDON   **Wharf**   Canalside garden
STAFFORD   **Home Croft**   Children's facilities and garden
STAFFORD   **Vine**   Children's facilities
TAMWORTH   **Gate**   Canalside garden
TRYSULL   **Plough**   Garden, play area

DERBYSHIRE (see also Maps 8 & 9)

COTON   **Black Horse**   Swings and lawn
COTON   **Elms**   Children's facilities
DERBY   **Mafeking**   Garden and bowling green
INGLEBY   **John Thompson**   Home brewery, riverside garden
MELBOURNE   **White Swan**   Children's facilities
REPTON   **Mount Pleasant**   Playground and children's facilities
SAWLEY (Long Eaton)   **Trent Navigation**   Views
SHARDLOW   **Malt Shovel**   Canalside
SHARDLOW   **Navigation**   Children's facilities, waterside garden
TICKNALL   **Chequers**   Garden with swings

MAP 5

NOTTINGHAMSHIRE (see also Map 9)

CROPWELL BISHOP **Lime Kiln**   Canalside
KINOULTON   **Nevill Arms**   Aviary, horse, swings
WILFORD (Nottingham)   **Ferry**   Riverside garden

LEICESTERSHIRE (see also Map 6)

CASTLE DONINGTON   **Cross Keys**   Children's facilities
LONG WHATTON   **Falcon**   Children's facilities
MEDBOURNE   **Horse & Trumpet**   Garden with bowling green
SKEFFINGTON   **Fox & Hounds**   Children's facilities and garden

MAP 6

BEDFORDSHIRE (see also Map 3)

1 UPPER DEAN   Three Compasses
(Riseley 346)
Charles Wells. Character 16th C thatched country pub. Meals (not Mon eve summer, Wed winter). Garden. Small room off main entrance used as family room.
On A45, NW of St Neots.

2 ROXTON   Royal Oak (Bedford 870361)
Charles Wells. Quaint turn-of-century pub. Bar meals daily. Garden with swings, see-saw, adventure castle. Children's room off garden with amusements. Traditional beer.
Off A428 in village between Bedford and St Neots.

3 TEMPSFORD   Anchor
(Biggleswade 40233)
Free House. Old one-time private house. Restaurant, bar meals. Garden with new children's room off it and main bar, or use of main entrance hall.
On A1 S of St Neots.

4 POTTON Everton Road   Rising Sun
(P 260231)
Free House. Victorian red-brick pub on green. Comprehensive bar snacks. Small garden. Family room in main entrance (games room). Traditional beer.
On B1042 E of Bedford.

HERTFORDSHIRE (see also Map 3)

5 HINXWORTH   Three Horseshoes
(Ashwell 2280)
Greene King. 200-year-old thatched village pub. Snacks. Garden. Old greenhouse off garden converted for family room. Traditional beer.
Off A1 N of Baldock.

6 BALDOCK Station Road   Old White Hart
Whitbread. Old coaching pub on main road. Meals. Small garden with children's shelter off it.
On A6141 in town centre.

7 WESTON (Halls Green)   Rising Sun
(W 236)
McMullen. Small 17th C one-time smallholding off the beaten track. Bar meals up to 9 pm daily. Large garden with birds and games. Family room off garden with games. Traditional beer.
W off B1031 N of Stevenage.

8 CHIPPING (nr Royston)   Countryman
(Royston 72616)
Free House. Small 17th C cottages (once used as the morgue). Restaurant evenings. Bar meals. Restaurant, off main bar, used as family room up to 7.30 pm. Traditional beer.
On A10 S of Royston.

ESSEX (see also Map 3)

9 GREAT BARDFIELD Vine Street   Vine
(Great Dunmow 810355)
Ridleys. Rebuilt pub on old site. Bar meals (not Sun lunch). Garden with aviary, children's room off car park with games. Traditional beer.
E off B1057 NW of Braintree.

SUFFOLK

10 HAVERHILL High Street   Queen's Head
(H 2026)
Tolly Cobbold. Victorian posting house. Meals. Dining room off car park used as family room. Traditional beer.
In town centre in SW corner of Suffolk.

11 HUNDON   Rose & Crown (H 261)
** Greene King. 16th C farm house. Bar meals. Garden, swings, see-saw. Family room off garden and main bar. Traditional beer.
E off A143 in straggling village centre NE of Haverhill.

12 CAVENDISH The Green   George
(Glemsford 280248)
Trumans. Old posting house. B & B, lunchtime snacks. Garden with family room off car park. Traditional beer.
On A1092 in pretty village centre, NW of Sudbury.

**13 LONG MELFORD Hall Street
George & Dragon** (LM 293)
Greene King. Old coaching posting house. Draw-in. Bar snacks. Patio yard with swings and donkeys. Family room off main bar or yard, with TV. Traditional beer.
On A1092 in town centre. S of Bury St Edmunds.

14 NAUGHTON   Wheeler's Arms
(Bildeston 740496)
Tolly Cobbold. 16th C thatched cottages (could be earlier). Basket meals. Family room off main bar. Traditional beer.

MAP 6

Off B1078 between Hadleigh and Bildeston. Off the beaten track.

15 WHATFIELD   Four Horseshoes
(Hadleigh 822103)
Tolly Cobbold. Old blacksmith's. Lunches (not Sun). Evening meals daily. Garden with adventure course and shelter. N off A1140 in village centre. Between Hadleigh and Bildeston.

16 PIN MILL   Boot & Oyster
(Woolverstone 224)
Tolly Cobbold. On water front. Lunches every day. Car park used as patio. Smoke room off passage used as family room. Traditional ale.
Off B1456 Shotley/Chelmondiston road towards sea.

17 BUNGAY St Mary's   Fleece (B 2192)
Adhams. Old coaching house. Lunches every day. Wide passage off main bar to car park with patio and seats for families. Traditional beer.
On A144 Hailsworth road, in town centre.

18 HUNTINGFIELD   Huntingfield Arms
(Ubbeston 320)
Free House. Stately private house Heveningham Hall. Lunches every day. Garden and village green. Family room off main bar until 7.30 pm. Traditional beer.
Off B1117 Hailsworth/Laxfield Road. Hard to find.

19 WINGFIELD   De La Pole
(Stradbrooke 666)
Free House. One-time church house much altered. Bar snacks. Garden. Children's room with games in porch off car park. Closed daytime Mon-Fri. Traditional beer.
N off B1118, 4m E of Diss.

20 WALSHAM-LE-WILLOWS   Six Bells
(WleW 726)
Greene King. 17th C cottage converted. B & B. Bar lunches (not Wed) and evenings every day. Garden, swings and slide. Family room off main entrance. Traditional beer.
S off A143 Bury/Diss road in village centre.

21 FRECKENHAM   Bell
Greene King. Small flint-built pub. Draw-in. Snacks. Garden with swings.Family room off main entrance. Traditional beer.

On B1102 on Cambs border in village centre.

22 WEST ROW (nr Mildenhall)
Jude's Ferry (Mildenhall 712277)
Free House. Private house by River Lark converted. Restaurant Tues to Sat, bar meals. Garden with slides. Use of saloon for families on wet days. Traditional beer.
W off A1101. Hard to find on byroads. N of Newmarket.

NORFOLK

23 BROCKDISH (nr Diss)   Old King's Head
** (Hoxne 510)
Free House. An old black and white coaching inn. B & B. Bar meals. Garden leading to river with boats and fishing. Family room off it with children's amusements. Traditional beer.
On A243 E of Diss.

24 BURGH ST PETER (nr Lowestoft)
Waveney Inn (Aldby 217)
Free House. Modern complex, camping, slipway. Basket meals. Garden with aviary. Children's room off garden with games. Closed 4 months winter. Traditional beer.
On A243, out in the wilds. Follow signs to end.

25 REEDHAM FERRY   Ferry
(Freethorpe 429)
Free House. Ancient ferrymen's house, pub still runs ferry. Meals all times. Garden lawns on waterside. Large children's area with games, and part of verandah at entrance. Traditional beer.
On B1140, N side of Broads.

26 BRUNDALL   White Horse
(Norwich 714878)
Watneys. Old world, restaurant, bar meals, garden with amusements. Children's room with games off main entrance. Traditional beer.
Off A47 through village to Broads. SE of Norwich.

27 SEA PALLING Wexham Road   Hale Inn
(Hooking 323)
Free House. 17th C house. B & B, bar meals (restaurant meals in winter). Garden. Children's room with games. Traditional beer.
Off B1159 in village centre between Yarmouth and Cromer.

MAP 6

28 WAYFORDBRIDGE   Wood Farm
(Stalham 81612)
Free House. Riverside complex with
shops and car park. Grill room and bar
meals. Patio with games, swings, etc.
Children's room off main entrance with
games. Traditional beer.
On A149 coast road NE of Norwich.

29 CAWSTON Eastgate   Gay Dunn (C 430)
Free House. One-time farmhouse. Bar
meals (except Wed eve). Garden with
swings. Family leisure room off car park
with numerous games. Traditional beer.
NW of Norwich road 1m out of village.

30 SOUTH CREEKE   Ostrich (SC 359)
Free House. 17th C coaching house. Bar
meals all times. Field at back. Old barn
converted to a family room with games
(sometimes used for meetings after
7.30 pm). Traditional beer.
On B1355 in village centre. NW of
Fakenham.

31 THORNHAM   Lifeboat (T 236)
Free House. Quaint 17th C rambling cottages converted. Meals lunchtime. Patio
at back with covered verandah/vinery, or
lounge entrance off the road. Traditional
beer.
Off A249, isolated, overlooking sea. NE
of Hunstanton.

**32 NORTH WOOTTON Station Road
Red Cat** (Castle Rising 244)
Free House. One-time Carr stone-built
farmhouse. B & B. Bar snacks. Large gardens with tennis courts. Small family
room off main entrance. Traditional beer.
Off A149 through Castle Rising.

33 GAYTON Lynn Road   Crown (G 252)
Greene King. One-time coaching house.
Bar meals except Sun. Garden with
swings with entry to large family room
(also off main bar). Traditional beer.
On A145 in village centre. E of Kings
Lynn.

34 CASTLE ACRE   Ostrich (CA 398)
Greene King. 16th C change house. Bar
meals all times. Garden with children's
play area. Family room off lawn or
through car park, adjacent main bar.
Traditional beer.
Off B1065 in village centre. N of
Swaffham.

35 HILBOROUGH   Swan
(Great Cressingham 380)

Free House. One-time shooting lodge.
B & B. Bar meals (except Mon eve).
Large garden and a family room off car
park entrance and through main bar.
Traditional beer.
On A1065 S of Swaffham.

36 THOMPSON (nr Watton)   Chequers
(Caston 360)
Free House. Picturesque, thatched 15th
C. Restaurant Wed to Sat eve. Bar
meals. Garden with swings, etc. Small
family room off car park or through main
low-ceiling beamed bar. Traditional ale.
Off B1075 Thetford/Watton road. Take
middle of three signs.

CAMBRIDGESHIRE

37 WATERBEACH Station Road   Star
(Cambridge 861287)
Greene King. Old bargees' pub. Lunches
Mon-Fri. Always something to eat. Gar-
den with animals and birds, games.
Small children's room off patio at back or
off main bar. Ringing the bull. Traditional
beer.
Linking A10 to A45, 4m NE of Cam-
bridge.

38 LODE   Cow & Hare
(Cambridge 811993)
Free House. Victorian brick pub. Meals.
Garden with swings. Children's room
with games off garden. Traditional ale.
Off B1102 at far end of pretty village
(now cul-de-sac). NE of Cambridge.

39 BOTTISHAM   White Swan
(Cambridge 811259)
Tolly Cobbold. One-time coaching
house. B & B, lunches (not Sun). Evening
meals (except Wed and Sun). Garden
with swings. Small conservatory (cold in
winter) off garden and main bar. Petrol.
Traditional beer.
On A1303, old Newmarket road. E of
Cambridge.

40 ST NEOTS New Street   Cannon
** (Huntingdon 73503)
Charles Wells. An old coaching posting
house. Draw-in. Snacks. Separate family
room off draw-in, part of old stables.
Traditional ale.
Off Square.

41 TILBROOK   Three Shuttles
(Kimbolton 244)
Charles Wells. Small farm cottages con-

MAP 6

verted. Snacks. Garden. Children/family room in games room off main bar or small room at back. Traditional beer. On A45 in village. NW of St Neots.

NORTHAMPTONSHIRE (see also Map 5)

42 THORPE WATERVILLE   Fox
(Clopton 274)
Charles Wells. Old stone cottage converted. Full meals every day. Garden. Children may use upstairs room off the pool room. Traditional beer.
On A505 S of Oundle.

LINCOLNSHIRE (see also Map 9)

43 BARHOLM   Five Horseshoes
(Greatford 238)
Free House. 19th C stone house of character. Meals (except Mon eve). Garden. Small hallway off car park to main bar used as family room. Traditional beer.
1½m N of A16 Stamford/Spalding road, in village centre.

44 PINCHBECK Northgate Road   Ship
* (Spalding 3792)
Watneys. Old bargees' house where coal was unloaded. B & B. Bar lunches and evening meals (children's portions).

Large garden with golf and swings. Family room off garden.
Off A16 on B1180, N of Spalding.

45 HOLBEACH   Rose & Crown (H 23941)
Free House. Typical old town pub. B & B. Meals at all times. Patio. Small hallway with tables off dining room for children. Traditional beer.
In town centre. E of Spalding.

46 SUTTERTON   Beridge Arms (S 272)
Home brewery. Victorian coaching house recently modernized. B & B. Snacks. Garden, family room. Traditional beer.
On A17 opposite church, S of Boston.

47 WAINFLEET High Street   Woolpack
(W 353)
Home brewery. One-time posting house. B & B. Bar meals. Large hall at end of passage used as family room with games.
On A52 in Square. SW of Skegness.

48 SKEGNESS Lumley Square   Lumley
(S 3536)
Hardy & Hanson. Large Victorian building with draw-in. Large family room off bar, with games.
On start of one-way system of A52 in town.

MAP 6
Other pubs to try

BUCKINGHAMSHIRE (see also Maps 3 & 5)

NORTH CRAWLEY   Cock   Children's facilities

BEDFORDSHIRE (see also Map 3)

BEDFORD   Angler's Rest   Gardens and donkeys
BEDFORD   Devonshire   Garden and play area
BEDFORD   Prince of Wales   Children's facilities
BEDFORD   Swan Inn   Riverside gardens and aviary
BOLNHURST   Old Plough   Moated garden
CARDINGTON (nr Bedford)   King's Arms   Garden playground, model-train rides
FANCOTT (Toddington)   Fancott Arms   Playground and model-train rides
KEMPSTON (nr Bedford)   Half Moon   Gardens and lawns
PULLOXHILL (nr Bedford)   Cross Keys   Lawns and garden
RIDGMONT (nr Bedford)   Rose & Crown   Lawns (Woburn Wild Life Park opposite)
WYBOSTON   Wait for the Waggon   Garden lawns

HERTFORDSHIRE (see also Map 3)

REED   Cabinet   Play area
ROYSTON   Old Bull   Children's facilities and garden

MAP 6

ESSEX (see also Map 3)

BARDFIELD END GREEN   **Butcher's Arms**   Gardens and cricket square
GREAT HENNY   **Swan**   Riverside and fishing
MANNINGTREE   **Crown**   Riverside
WETHERSFIELD   **Brewery Tavern**   Children's facilities
WETHERSFIELD   **Dog**   Games room

SUFFOLK

ALDRINGHAM (Leiston)   **Parrot & Punchbowl**   Garden, outside and inside facilities
BECCLES   **Loaves & Fishes**   Waterside with moorings
BILDESTON   **Crown**   Play area
BRANDESTON   **Queen's Head**   Garden and camping area
BRIDGE STREET   **Rose & Crown**   Children's facilities and garden
BROME   **Oaks Mere**   In own grounds
FLEMPTON   **Greyhound**   Garden and village green
GREAT BRICETT   **Red Lion**   Alcoholic donkey
LOWESTOFT   **Foxburrow**   Peacocks and pet foxes
NEWBOURN   **Fox**   Garden and bowls
OULTON BROAD (Lowestoft)   **George Burrow**   Garden and indoor facilities
REDGRAVE   **Cross Keys**   Garden and village green
RENDHAM (nr Saxmundham)   **White Horse**   Play area
SAXMUNDHAM   **Queen's Head**   Garden and indoor facilities
SAXSTEAD   **Volunteer**   Village green and windmill
SHOTLEY GATE   **Bristol Arms**   Waterside with views
SOMERLEYTON (Lowestoft)   **Duke's Head**   Garden and indoor facilities
SOUTHWOLD   **King's Head**   Children's facilities
WALBERSWICK   **Bell**   Children's facilities and play area near beach
WOOLPIT   **Bull**   Attractive lawns
WORLINGWORTH   **Swan**   Children's facilities and garden

NORFOLK

BELTON   **King's Head**   Garden and indoor facilities
BLAKENEY   **Manor**   Children's facilities and garden
CAISTER   **Never Turn Back**   Garden and indoor facilities in summer
CAISTER   **Ship**   Garden and summerhouse (in summer)
COLTISHALL   **Red Lion**   Play area
CROMER   **Old Red Lion**   Children's facilities
CROMER   **Wellington**   Children's facilities
DISS   **Sun Inn**   Play area and fishing
GELDESTON   **Locks**   Play area, isolated, sometimes marooned
GELDESTON   **Wherry**   Riverside garden
GORLESTON (Great Yarmouth)   **Oddfellows Arms**   Garden and indoor facilities
GREAT MOULTON   **Fox & Hounds**   Garden and indoor facilities
GREAT YARMOUTH   **Nelson**   Sea front, patio, garden
GREAT YARMOUTH   **Oliver Twist**   Play area
HEYDON   **Earl Arms**   Garden and village green
HOLT   **Bluebell**   Village green
HOPTON (Great Yarmouth)   **Turnstone**   Patio and indoor facilities
INGOLDISTHORPE   **Manor**   Private grounds
KELLING   **Pine Court**   In own grounds
LODDON   **Swan**   Patio and indoor facilities
NORTH WALSHAM   **Scarborough Hill House**   Children's facilities and 4-acre grounds
NORWICH   **Ferry Boat**   Riverside garden
NORWICH   **Plasterer's Arms**   Children's facilities
ORMESBY ST MICHAEL (Great Yarmouth)   **Eel's Foot**   Riverside garden, play area, indoor room, swings

MAP 6

OVERSTRAND **Overstrand Court** Children's facilities, own woodland area
RUNHAM VAUXHALL **Suspension Bridge** Garden with outside and inside facilities
SALTHOUSE **Lodge** Own grounds
SCRABY **California** Garden, play area, indoor room in summer
TITCHWELL **Three Horseshoes** Children's facilities and garden
WATTON **Hare & Barrel** Children's facilities and garden
WEST RUNTON **Village Inn** Children's facilities, garden with amusements
WYMONDHAM **Queen's Head** Garden and indoor facilities

CAMBRIDGESHIRE

BARRINGTON **Royal Oak** On village green
BUCKDEN (St Neots) **Spread Eagle** Garden, play area
CAMBRIDGE **Grants** Riverside with moorings
CAMBRIDGE **Spade & Bucket** Riverside garden
CAMBRIDGE (Chesterton Rd) **Rob Roy** Riverside garden
CHESTERTON (nr Cambridge) **Green Dragon** Riverside
EARITH **Crown** Riverside
ELTISLEY (St Neots) **Leeds Arms** Village green
FEN DITTON **Plough** Riverside garden
HOLYWELL **Old Ferry Boat** England's oldest inn, riverside
ORWELL **Chequers** Indoor facilities
PETERBOROUGH **Green Keeper** Garden with pitch and putt
RAMSEY **Lion** Children's facilities and garden
REACH **Dyke's End** Village green
SAWSTON **Black Bull** Garden and folk room
SOHAM **Cherry Tree** Playground
TRUMPINGTON **Unicorn** Fish pond

NORTHAMPTONSHIRE (see also Map 5)

STOKE DOYLE **Shuckburgh Arms** Children's facilities and garden

LEICESTERSHIRE (see also map 5)

COTTESMORE **Sun** Children's facilities and garden

LINCOLNSHIRE (see also Map 9)

CONINGSBY **White Bull** Children's facilities, garden, swings
CONINGSBY **White Swan** Children's facilities and garden
EDENHAM **Five Bells** Children's facilities and garden
GRANTHAM **Granby** Children's facilities
LEADENHAM **George** Children's facilities
LONG SUTTON **Bull** Children's facilities
SKEGNESS **County** Children's facilities
SLEAFORD **Nags Head** Children's facilities
SURFLEET **Mermaid** Children's facilities and riverside garden
TATTERSHALL **Fortescue Arms** Children's facilities

MAP 7

DYFED (see also Map 4)

1 BORTH Railway (B 348)
Free House. Victorian country-town pub.
B & B. Restaurant open every day. Bar
meals. Garden. Large summer room for
children with amusements and, in
winter, use of separate lounge off main
bar. Traditional beer. Closed Sunday.
On A4353 in town centre.

2 TALYBONT White Lion (T 245)
Banks. One-time coaching stage. B & B.
Restaurant every day summer, not Sun
winter. Bar meals. Garden with
children's hut, TV for wet or winter
days. Traditional beer.
On A487 in village centre.

POWYS

3 LLANDINAM Lion (Caersws 233)
Free House. One-time farm, still with
poultry etc, backing on to River Severn.
B & B. Restaurant (bookable except high
season). Home cooked bar meals. Gar-
den. Children's room off main entrance.
Traditional ale. 4m fishing rights.
On A470 in village.

4 LLANFAIR CAEREINION Black Lion
(LlC 207)
Greenall Whitley. One-time coaching
stage. Lunches Mon-Sat (Sun by order).
Bar meals evenings. Garden with swings
and frame. Children's/family room off
main passage. Traditional beer. Market
day Tuesday.
Just off A458 in town centre.

5 LLANGADFAN Cann Office (Ll 202)
Border. One of Wales's oldest sites,
dated 1310. B & B. Bar meals. Garden.
Family room off garden at back. Fishing
rights.
On A458, isolated.

GWYNEDD

6 DOLGELLAU Bridge Street Stag
(D 422533)
Burtonwood. 18th C tap room to coach-
ing stage house, recently modernized.
Roadside parking. Light bar meals. Patio.
Family room upstairs at back (likely to be
moved downstairs). Traditional beer.
Closed Sun all day.
On A470 in town centre on one-way
system.

7 MAENTWROG Oakeley Arms (M 277)
* Free House. 17th C ferry/coaching
house. Accommodation. Restaurant eve
only. Bar meals. Garden. Children's room
off bar entrance and children's/ family
restaurant opposite. Traditional ale.
Closed Sunday.
On A487.

8 FFESTINIOG Pengwern Arms (F 2722)
Free House. Coaching stage and black-
smith's. B & B. Substantial bar meals.
Garden. Large children's/family room off
entrance with fish tank. Closed Sunday.
On A470 in village centre.

9 RHYD DDU Cwellyn Arms
* (Beddgelert 267)
Greenall Whitley. At foothills of Snow-
don in small village. B & B. Snacks lunch-
time. Basket evening meals (seasonal).
Garden. Family room off passageway
until 8 pm. Closed Sunday.
On A4085.

10 NANT PERIS Vaynol Arms
(Llanberis 284)
Robinsons. One-time drovers' pub with
water wheel (disused) alongside. B & B.
Bar snacks. Play area. Family room with
pool table. Traditional beer. Closed
Sundays.
On A4086 beneath Snowdon.

11 CAPEL CURIG Tyn-y-Coed (CC 231)
Free House. One-time private house/
farm converted. Accommodation. Res-
taurant evenings. Bar meals. Garden.
Family room off main entrance.
On A5 Bettws-y-Coed side of village.

12 BETTWS-Y-COED Silver Fountain
(BC 341)
Free House. B & B. Restaurant. Bar
meals. Garden. Children's/family room
off main bar.
On A5 E of town.

CLWYD

13 ABERGALE Water Street Castle
(A 824068)
Bass. Typical Victorian pub. Roadside
parking. Snacks. Patio yard at back with
part covered for wet weather. Traditional beer.
In town centre near church.

14 RHYL West Parade Schooner
** (R 53124)

MAP 7

Allied. Modern seaside pub. Car park, limited space. Snacks. Patio in front and large children's room upstairs for summer, seating in verandah in winter. On sea front at west end.

15 RUTHIN Anchor (R 2873)
Bass. 3-storey stucco front with shutters. B & B. Bar snacks. Patio. Family room off the main bar, used as pool room. Traditional ale. In town centre on A494.

16 GRAIGFECHAN Three Pigeons (Ruthin 3178) Free House. Old drovers' pub dated 1777. Light snacks. Patio. Barn converted to large family room. Traditional beer. On B5429 2m E of A525.

17 GYFELIA Waggoners (Ruabon 3580)

** Border. Old stone building. Bar snacks. Attractive garden and bowling green with swings, slide, see-saw. Back patio covered for bad weather. Traditional beer. On B5426 near Eyton.

18 CYNWYD Blue Lion (Corwen 2106)
Marstons. 17th C coaching stage. Bar snacks. Garden. Children's/family room off main entrance. Traditional beer. Off A5 S 2m on B4401.

19 PONTFADOG Graig (Clen Ceriog 712)
Free House. Private house converted, with valley views. Bar lunches daily and evening meals. Patio. Children's room off the patio in converted outhouse. Traditional beer. Off A5 off B4500, hard to find and watch the bend.

MAP 7
Other pubs to try

DYFED (see also Map 4)

BORTH Friendship Children's facilities and garden
MEIFOD King's Head Children's facilities and garden
SARN (nr Newtown) Penrhyn Arms Swings and sandpit

GWYNEDD

ABERDARON Ty-Neydd Backs on to beach
ABERSOCH White House Aviary and garden
BARMOUTH Tal-y-Don Garden and open-sided shelter
CORRIS UCHAF Dulas Valley Children's facilities, garden and views
EDERN (nr Nefyn) Ship Children's facilities
LLWYNGWRIL Garthangharad Children's facilities and garden
PENRHYNDEUDRAETH Port Merrion Quayside in unique setting
TUDWEILIOG Lion Lawns and swings

ANGLESEY

BANGOR-ON-DEE Royal Oak Riverside views
BULL BAY Trecastell Cliff-top garden, views over sands
GLYNGARTH (Menai Bridge) Gazelle Waterside, own landing stage
HOLYHEAD Rose & Crown Children's facilities
TREARDDUR BAY (nr Holyhead) Trearddur Bay Overlooking sea

CLWYD

BRYNFORD (nr Hollywell) Crooked Horn Garden with views
BWLCH-Y-CIBAU Cross Keys Play area and swings
BYLCHAU Sportsman's Arms Countryside, highest in Wales
CAERGWRLE Bridge Inn Riverside
CONNAH'S QUAY Old Quay House Riverside

MAP 7

ERBISTOCK   **Boat**   Waterside
GRONANT (nr Prestatyn)   **Bells**   Play area in monks' resthouse
HALKYN   **Britannia**   Swings and pets' corner
LLANARMON-YN-LAL   **Raven**   Children's facilities and garden
LLANGOLLEN   **Bridgend**   Riverside, children's facilities
MARCHWIEL   **Red Lion**   Play area and lawns
NERCWYS   **Owain Glyndwr**   Garden with views
RUABON   **Duke of Wellington**   Lawns
RHYL   **White Horse**   Children's facilities in passageway
WAEN ST ASPETH   **Farmer's Arms**   Children's facilities

MAP 8

CHESHIRE

1 NANTWICH Welsh Row
Oddfellows Arms (N 64758)
Ind Coope. 17th C pub with name changed from Boot & Shoe. Roadside parking. Lunches Mon-Sat. Beer garden with swings, back yard covered and used as family room. Traditional beer. On A51 on N side of town.

2 TARPORLEY High Street Rising Sun
(T 2423)
Robinsons. 17th C minor coaching stage. Restaurant evenings (not Sun). Bar snacks. Sun lunch. Children use two rambling rooms off main entrance. Traditional beer.
On A49 in town centre, SE of Chester.

3 DELAMERE Vale Royal Abbey Arms
(Sandiway 2747)
Watneys. 16th C monks hospice from Whitegate Abbey. Lunches (not Sat). Snacks evenings. Large garden with swings. Family room/snug off the main entrance. Traditional beer.
On A556 at crossroad B5152 on edge of forest. SW of Norwich.

4 FRODSHAM Main Street Golden Lion
(F 32179)
Samuel Smith. Coaching house in Square. Roadside parking. Lunches Mon-Sat. Light snacks other times. Small smoke room used as family room and lounge lunchtime. Traditional beer.
On A56 1½m from J12/14 M52.

5 MIDDLEWICH Boar's Head (M 3191)
Robinsons. Large Victorian pub. B & B. Lunches Mon-Fri. Snacks evenings and weekends. Large family room off passage with TV and daytime use of pool room. Traditional beer.
On A54 town ring road. N of Crewe.

6 PEOVER SUPERIOR (nr Knutsford)
* **Whipping Stock** (Lower Peover 2332)
Samuel Smith. Picturesque 15th C farmhouse and court, with place of punishment outside. Bar meals all times. Large garden with numerous amusements and family room off the garden.
On A50 at Stocks Lane. 3m S of Knutsford.

7 BUGLAWTON Robin Hood
(Congleton 3616)
Marstons. 18th C court-house farm. Bar snacks (except Mon eve). Garden. Family room off car park up to 8 pm. Traditional beer.
On A54 E of Congleton, 2m.

8 BUGLAWTON Church House
(Congleton 2466)
Robinsons. Modern between-wars pub taking licence from old pub. Bar meals (not Sun). Garden. Large family room off main entrance. Traditional beer.
On A54 E of Congleton. 1m.

9 HIGHER SUTTON Ryles Arms
(Sutton 2244)
Watneys. One-time 16th C farm. Bar snacks all times. Small garden. Family room off main bar up to 8pm.
N on byroad off A54 half-way Congleton/ Buxton.

10 WINCLE Wild Boar (W 219)
Robinsons. One-time sheep farm on edge of Dales. Bar meals (except Mon night). Lawn. 2 family rooms, one up to 8pm, off the main bar. Traditional ale.
On A54 E of Congleton, half-way to Buxton.

11 BOLLINGTON (Kerridge) Lord Clyde
(B 73202)
Greenall Whitley. Old private mill cottage industry now a pub. Family room off entrance passage and main bar. Traditional beer.
Kerridge road off A523 ½m. 3m N of Macclesfield.

STAFFORDSHIRE (see also Map 5)

12 NEWCASTLE-UNDER-LYME High Street
Golden Lion (NuL 616115)
Bass. Victorian pub in modern surrounds with preservation order. Paying car park. Snacks all times. Yard at back covered, making a family room, with play area beyond. Traditional beer.
In town centre, on shopping precinct.

DERBYSHIRE (see also Maps 5 & 9)

13 CAT & FIDDLE (Wildboarclough,
* **nr Macclesfield) Cat & Fiddle**
(Buxton 3364)
Robinsons. England's second highest pub, 1,690ft with panoramic views. Once Earl of Derby's shooting lodge. Full extensive meals throughout the bars. Moorland playground. Large room through main bar used as family room in

MAP 8

bad weather. Traditional beer.
On A537 4m from Buxton.

14 LITTON   Red Lion (Tideswell 871458)
Free House. 17th C building of stone.
Bar meals Thurs, Fri, Sat, Sun, day and
evenings. Home cooking. Patio. Family/
children's room through passage available until 8.30pm (closed Mon, Tues,
Wed, daytime).
½m off B6049 on village green. NW of
Bakewell.

15 BRADWELL   Bowling Green
 * (Hope Valley 20450)
Free House. Typical Dales pub. Lunches
daily. Evenings Fri-Sun. Snacks other
times. Goats & farm animals, swings
etc. in wild garden. Family room with
bird until 9.30pm.
¼m off B6064 in village centre. E of
Whaley Bridge.

16 EDALE   Old Nag's Head
 * (Hope Valley 70212)
Free House. 16th C cottages converted.
Limited meals all times. Patio. Stables
converted to family room with own ice-
cream, soft drinks bar. Traditional ale.
4m N off the A625 high up in the National
Park Dales.

17 EDALE   Ramblers (Hope Valley 71268)
Free House. Built as a hotel in 1900 in
local stone. B & B. Full meals all times.
Garden and field with playground and
animals. Hikers' room and family room
off main entrance. Traditional beer.
4m off A625. NE of Buxton.

GREATER MANCHESTER

**18 BAMFORD (nr Bury) Old Bury Road
Hare & Hounds** (Heywood 69189)
Thwaites. 2 cottages converted.
Lunches Mon-Fri. Snacks weekends.
Patio. Family room at back off lounge bar
in games room until 8pm. Traditional
beer.
On B6222 NE of Bolton.

19 AFFETSIDE   Pack Horses
(Tottington 3802)
Hydes. 17th C coaching inn on older
site. Bar meals every day and evening.
Garden. Families in games room until
8pm. Traditional beer.
Just off A676 Old Watling Street. N of
Bolton.

LANCASHIRE

20 HASKAYNE Rosemary Lane   Ship
(Ormskirk 840572)
Allied. Old bargees' canalside pub. Lun-
ches Mon-Fri (occ. w/es). Garden with
numerous amenities. Large family room
with machine games leading off garden.
Off A5147 Southport road. SE of
Southport.

21 LONGTON Marsh Lane   Dolphin
(L 612032)
Free House. Tiny farm, wild-fowling
associations. Farm animals. Small family
room off main entrance. Quaint servery.
Traditional beer.
Off A59 through Longton, 1¼m towards
estuary.

22 CLIFTON   Windmill (Kirkham 686124)
Free House. Old windmill (without pad-
dles) converted. Meals all times. Garden.
Barn through main bar as family room.
Traditional beer.
½m N off A583 Blackpool road by
Lytham St Anne's turn-off.

23 CHIPPING   Talbot (C 206)
Boddingtons. One-time farm. Bar
snacks. Garden with entrance to family
room (or through main bar). Traditional
beer.
In wilds, off beaten track, NE of Preston,
in village centre.

24 BARNACRE (nr Garstang)   Kenlis Arms
(Garstang 3307)
Free House. One-time hunting lodge for
Barnacre estate. B & B. Bar snacks. Gar-
den. Family room opposite bar in main
entrance. Traditional beer.
E off A6 south end of Garstang.

25 OAKENCLOUGH   Moor Cock
(Garstang 2130)
Free House. One-time farm house. Meals
day and evening. Patio. Families use
coffee room off road and through main
bar. Traditional beer.
4m off A6 in Garstang, high in Bleasdale
Moor.

26 DOLPHINHOLME   Fleece
(Forton 791233)
Mitchells. 20 acres of land, still part of
pub, once farm. Light snacks. Small gar-
den. Children allowed in entrance hall.
Traditional beer.
At crossroads on Chipping road, 3m from
J33 M6 through Bay Horse.

MAP 8

27 FORTON New Holly (F 791568)
Thwaites. Victorian roadside pub. B & B.
Bar lunches and evening meals daily.
Field and patio. Room off main entrance
used as family room. Traditional beer.
On A6 S of Lancaster, 2m from J33 M6.

28 BAY HORSE (nr Lancaster) Bay Horse
(Forton 791204)
Mitchells. 17th C coaching house.
B & B. Bar meals. Patio at back with
games room used as family room off it.
Traditional beer.
Just off A6, ½m from J33 M6 on old
road.

29 GLASSON DOCK Caribou
(Galgate 751356)
Thwaites. 18th C chandlers supplying
ships. B & B. Bar snacks. Large concert
room used as family room. Traditional
beer.
At end of B5290 on quayside. 5m W from
J33 M6.

30 SNATCHAMS (Heaton-in-Oxcliffe)
Golden Ball (Lancaster 63317)
Mitchell. Isolated on marshes, 16th C
waterside pub (cut off by high tide flood-
ing). Roadside parking. Snacks, garden
view over estuary. Small family room
through bar upstairs with specially made
furniture.
1¼m off A5890 Overton road to Morecambe.

31 TATHAM Bridge (Horby 21326)
Mitchells. Old smallholding of yester-
year. B & B. Bar meals day and evening.
Garden with amusements. Small family
room off main passage opposite bar.
Traditional beer.
On B6480 in village centre. NE of Lan-
caster.

WEST YORKSHIRE

33 HINCHLIFFE MILLS (Holmbridge,
Holmfirth) Bare Knuckle Boys
(Holmfirth 2329)
Thwaites. One-time prize-fighting HQ up
to 1923. Bar meals. Snacks. Family room
upstairs in room once gym. Traditional
beer.
On B6024 Woodhead road.

34 MARSDEN Olive Branch
(Huddersfield 844487)
Bass. Oldest pub in village. 18th C
stone. Bar lunches Mon-Fri. Snacks

other times. Families use dining room off
main bar. Traditional beer.
On A62, Huddersfield side of village.

35 UPTON (nr Mirfield) Traveller's Rest
(Mirfield 4938981)
Allied. One time farm with fine views.
Lunches Mon-Fri. Garden with amuse-
ments. Large family room off car park.
Traditional beer.
N off A642 S of Mirfield. 4m from J25
M62.

36 KEELHAM Brown Cow
(Bradford 833077)
Allied. Stone building once post office.
Bar meals day and evening. Garden with
swings etc. Large family room off car
park with own toilets outside. Traditional
beer.
At junction B6145/A644. S of Denholme.

37 HIGH ELDWICK Dick Hudson
(Bingley 2554)
Alied. Isolated farmhouse converted.
Lunches (limited Sun, Mon). Garden with
swings and house. Large family room,
fine views overlooking valley. Traditional
beer.
High above Bingley, to NE on minor
roads.

38 ADDINGHAM Fleece (A 830491)
* Allied. Rough stone, rambling 16th C
character village inn. Lunches Mon-Sat.
½ acre of ground at back. 2 excellent
family rooms with amusements available. Traditional beer.
On A65 in village centre. NW of Ilkley.

NORTH YORKSHIRE (see also Map 9)

39 SNAYGILL (nr Bradley) Bay Horse
** (Skipton 2449)
Allied. Old farm coaching stage. Dining
room, bar lunches, snacks evenings.
Garden playground. Large children's/
family room at far end of main bar, or
from garden. Own toilets.
On A629 S of Skipton.

40 AUSTWICK Cross Streets
(Clapham 206)
Free House. One-time rough-stone farm
with fine views from Backham Brow.
B & B. Bar meals. Long verandah for
families and games room through main
bar.
On A65 isolated in Pennines. NE of
Settle.

MAP 8

41 STAINFORTH   Craven Heifer
(Settle 2599)
Thwaites. Old packhorse stage house.
B & B. Bar meals all times. Garden along-
side river. Large family room off main
passage until 9pm. Traditional ale.
¼m off B6479 in village centre. N of
Settle.

42 HORTON-IN-RIBBLESDALE (nr Settle)
Helwith Bridge (Horton 220)
Free House. 18th C riverside pub with
views. B & B. Meals. Garden with goats
and peacocks. Breakfast room used as
family room to 8.30pm. Traditional beer.
Just off B6479, in hamlet high up in Pennines. N of Settle.

43 BELLERBY   Cross Keys
(Wensleydale 22256)
Marstons. Typical old village pub. B & B,
snacks. Village green. Children's/family
room off the car park. Traditional beer.
On A6108 in picturesque village centre.
N of Leyburn.

44 HARMBY   Pheasant
(Wensleydale 22223)
Free House. 16 C farmhouse. Caravan
site. Bar snacks. Field and hunters.
Family room off main entrance until
9pm. Traditional beer.
On A684 at edge of village. E of Leyburn.

CUMBRIA (see also Map 10)

45 CASTERTON   Pheasant
(Kirkby Lonsdale 71230)
Free House. One-time coaching stage.
B & B. Restaurant. (Sun lunch and
evenings). Bar meals. Garden. Small
lobby at main entrance used as a family
room.
On A683 in village centre, 2m N of Kirkby
Lonsdale.

46 BARBON   Barbon (B 233)
Free House. Georgian farmhouse converted. B & B (4-poster bed). Restaurant
every evening. Bar meals. Beer garden.
Family room in well-furnished lounge off
main bar until 8pm.
1m E off A683 Cragg Hill on Pennines in
village centre.

47 HALE   King's Arms (Milnthorpe 3203)
Mitchells. 18th C coaching stage. B & B.
Bar meals available day and evening.
Garden and bowling green. Large family
room at top of stairs through main bar.

Traditional beer.
On A6, 2m S of Milnthorpe. 5m from
J35/36, M6.

48 CARTMEL Market Place   King's Arms
(C 220)
Whitbread. 17th C market hospice.
Roadside parking. Bar snacks lunchtime.
Patio in front. Family room off passage
opposite bar (used occasionally for meet-
ings). Traditional beer.
Off B5278 in village centre. W of Grange-
over-Sands.

49 GRIZEBECK   Greyhound
(Kirkby-in-Furness 224)
Free House. Victorian farm. B & B. Bar
meals. Family room off main entrance to
bar. Traditional beer.
Just off A595 in village centre. N of
Ulveston.

50 HAWKSHEAD Main Street   Sun (H 236)
Bass. Minor posting coach house of the
18th C enlarged. Public park nearby.
Substantial bar meals. Large family room
off main bar.
In village centre off B528. Off A593 SW
of Ambleside.

51 OUTGATE   Outgate (Hawkshead 413)
Hartleys. 18th C causeway cottages
converted. B & B. Bar lunches. Families
allowed in large front room in day (not
evening). Traditional beer.
On B5281, a small hamlet. On W side of
Lake Windermere.

52 TROUTBECK   Queen's Head
(Ambleside 2174)
Free House. 17th C farmhouse. Restaurant (summer only). Snacks (full
meals in winter). Patio. Children's/
family room off main bar used as games
room. Traditional beer.
On A592 in village centre. N of Windermere.

53 AMBLESIDE Smithy Brow   Golden Rule
(A 2257)
Hartleys. 17th C cottages and coaching
house. Draw-in, limited parking. Snacks
Mon-Fri. Patio with birds and rabbits.
Small games room used by families
either side of bar up to 8pm. Traditional
beer.
On Kirkstone road off A591, N end of
town.

54 KIRKSTONE PASS   Kirkstone Pass
(Ambleside 3248)

MAP 8

Free House. One of England's highest inns, 1,500ft. 17th C isolated coaching house with grand views. B & B. Bar meals 365 days and nights a year. 8¼ acres of wilds. Family room off main bar. On A592. NE of Ambleside.

55 GRASMERE Traveller's Rest (G 378)
Vaux. 17th C coaching house with views. B & B. Bar snacks. Meals in evening. Family room off main bar until 8pm. Traditional beer.
On A591 1m N. Grasmere in valley.

56 GREAT LANGDALE Dungeon Ghyll Stickle Barn (Langdale 356)
Free House. 18th C barn, converted in 1974, with views. Hot bar meals (late starting each season). Patio. Alcove off main bar for family room. Traditional beer.
On B5243 road to mountains. W of Grasmere.

57 ESKDALE Bower House (E 244)
Free House. 12th C site of old farm. Accommodation. Restaurant, bar meals. Garden, putting green. Small family room off main bar. Traditional beer.
2m off A595 in hamlet.

58 ESKDALE King George IV (E 262)
Free House. Georgian farmhouse with views. Meals day and evening. Patio. Family games room at back of pub off

2nd car park. Traditional beer.
4½m off A595, isolated at junction.

59 RAVENGLASS Ratty Arms (R 676)
Free House. Part of the Railway Station. Miniature railway and museum opposite. BR trains run through. Meals all times. Patio. Children are allowed in railway verandah off main bar. Traditional beer.
½m off A595 in village.

60 BECKERMET Royal Oak (B 551)
Free House. 18th C cottages converted. B & B. Meals. Garden off the car park. Family room off main bar. Traditional beer.
2m off A595 in village centre. S of Whitehaven.

61 NATEBY Black Bull
(Kirkby Stephen 71588)
Marstons. 17th C typical beamed village pub. B & B. Bar meals day and evening. Snug room off lounge used as family room.
On B6270 in village centre. S of Brough.

62 BROUGH Main Street George (B 357)
Free House. One-time coaching stage. B & B. Bar snacks. Garden. Small snug with TV used as family room off main bar.
¼m off A66 in town centre. SW of Appleby.

MAP 8
Other pubs to try

CHESHIRE

ACTON BRIDGE Leigh Arms Bowling green, riverside
ALDERLEY EDGE Moss Rose Garden and bowling green
ALPHRAHAM Traveller's Rest Garden and canal
ASTBURY (Congleton) Egerton Arms Garden, swings, slides, goats, rabbits
AUDLEM Bridge Canalside
CHESTER Red House Terrace on riverside with moorings
CHURCH LAWTON Red Bull Canalside garden
EASTHAM (Wirral) Eartham Ferry Riverside
FARNDON Nag's Head Swings and playground
HALEBARNS Bull's Head Garden and bowling green
LOWER PEOVER Bells Children's area and old churchyard
LYMM Jolly Threshers Garden and bowling green
MIDDLEWICH Newton Brewery Canalside garden
MOORE (nr Warrington) Red Lion Canalside
NANTWICH Oddfellows Play area and garden
RODE HEATH Broughton Arms Canalside garden
SANDBACH George Garden and bowling green
TATTENHALL Sportsman's Garden and bowling green
TILSTON Fox & Hounds Swings

MAP 8

STAFFORDSHIRE (see also Map 5)

ALTONSFIELD **George** Garden and village green
BAGNALL (Stoke-on-Trent) **Stafford Arms** Village green
BURSLEM (Greenhead Street) **Foaming Quart** Play area
CELLARHEAD **Hope & Anchor** Play area
CHEDDLETON (Leek) **Boat** Canalside
CONSALL **Black Lion** Canalside, garden
HANLEY (Stoke-on-Trent) **Golden Cup** Views
LEEK **Churnet Valley** Play area
LEEK **Red Lion** Children's facilities
LONGNOR (nr Buxton) **Old Cheshire Cheese** Children's facilities
LONGSDON **Hollybush** Children's facilities, canalside
MADELEY (nr Newcastle) **Offley Arms** Play area
MEIR (Stoke-on-Trent) **Station** Play area, putting green
NEWCASTLE-UNDER-LYME **Golden Lion** Children's facilities
STOCKTON BROOK (nr Stoke-on-Trent) **Rose & Crown** Play area
WHITMORE (Newcastle-under-Lyme) **Sheet Anchor** Garden with swings

DERBYSHIRE (see also Maps 5 & 9)

ASHFORD **Bull's Head** Farmyard
EARL STERNDALE **Quiet Woman** Village green
HOPE **Cheshire Cheese** Children's facilities and garden

GREATER MANCHESTER

ASHTON-ON-MERSEY **Old Plough** Children's facilities
ASPULL **Kirkley's Hall** Canalside garden
ASPULL **Queens Head** Garden on village green
BOLTON **Howcroft** Garden and bowling green
CHEADLE HULME **Junction** Children's facilities and garden
DENSHAW **Porters Arms** Play area, garden, views
GATHURST **Navigation** Canalside garden
HYDE **Grapes** Play area, bowling green
INCE-IN-MAKERFIELD **Park** Garden with bowling green
LOWTON **Jolly Carter** Play area
MANCHESTER CITY (Duci Street) **Jolly Angler** Children's facilities
MARPLE BRIDGE **George** Boating
MILNROW **Waggon** Children's facilities
RINGWAY (Manchester Airport) **Airport** Lawns, play area backing on airport
ROMILEY **Friendship** Garden with swings and slide
ROYTON **Puckersley** Play area, garden with views

MERSEYSIDE

BILLINGE **Holts Arms** Garden and bowling green
LYDIATE **Running Horses** Canalside garden
SOUTHPORT **Zetland** Garden and bowling green
THATTO HEATH **Brown Edge** Bowling green

LANCASHIRE

BILSBORROW **White Bull** Canalside garden
BLACKBURN **Navigation** Canalside
CHARNOCK RICHARD (nr Ouseley) **Bowling Green** Play area
CHORLEY **Spinners** Canalside garden

MAP 8

DALTON (nr Parbold)   **Prince William**   Views and garden
GARSTANG   **Crown**   Bowling green
HALSALL (nr Ormskirk)   **Saracen's Head**   Canalside
HAPTON   **Bridge House**   Canalside
HESKIN GREEN (nr Chorley)   **Brook House**   Play area
HESTBANK   **Hestbank**   Canalside
MELLING (nr Ormskirk)   **Melling Hall**   Own grounds
MIDDLETON-IN-LONSDALE   **Middleton Fell**   Play area
MORECAMBE   **Grosvenor**   Garden play area
MORECAMBE   **York**   Children's facilities and garden
PLEASINGTON   **Railway**   Garden and bowling green
POULTON-LE-FYLDE   **River Wyre**   Playground
SCARISBRICK (Southport)   **Heatons Bridge**   Canalside garden
SCOTFORTH (nr Lancaster)   **Boot & Shoe**   Bowling green and children's area
SKELMERSDALE   **Hare & Hounds**   Garden and bowling green
WALTON-LE-DALE   **Bridge**   Riverside garden
WHITTLE (nr Chorley)   **Howard Arms**   Playing fields and bowling green
WREA GREEN (nr Kirkham)   **Grapes**   Garden, nr village green

WEST YORKSHIRE (see also Map 9)

BRIGHOUSE   **Black Horse**   Great Danes, pets and rabbits
ELLAND   **Collier's Arms**   Canalside garden
LAYCOCK (nr Keighley)   **Turkey**   Garden and home brewery opposite
LUMB   **Hargrave's Arms**   Playground opposite
MARSDEN   **Railway**   Views and canal

NORTH YORKSHIRE (see also Map 9)

AYSGARTH   **George & Dragon**   Children's facilities and garden
EAST MARTON   **Cross Keys**   Canalside
HIGHER BENTHAM   **Royal Oak**   Children's facilities and garden
KIRBY HILL   **Bluebell**   Play area, caravans, camping
LOWER BENTHAM   **Punch Bowl**   Children's facilities and riverside
MIDDLEHAM   **Black Swan**   Children's facilities

CUMBRIA (see also Map 10)

ARNSIDE   **Albion**   Estuary views
DALTON-IN-FURNESS   **Horse & Jockey**   Children's facilities
DALTON-IN-FURNESS   **White Horse**   Children's facilities
FAR SAWREY   **Sawrey**   Children's facilities
GRANGE-OVER-SANDS   **Crown**   Children's facilities and garden
HAVERTHWAITE (nr Woolverton)   **Angler's Arms**   Lakeside railway opposite
KIRKBY-IN-FURNESS   **Commercial**   Children's facilities
KIRKBY LONSDALE   **Whoop Hall**   Own grounds and camping
MIDDLETON   **Swan**   Children's facilities
NEWBY BRIDGE   **Swan**   Riverside garden
RAMPSIDE   **Clarkes Arms**   Overlooking sea
ROSTHWAITE   **Scarfell**   Children's facilities and riverside
WINDERMERE   **Stott's Hall**   Lakeside private grounds

MAP 9

DERBYSHIRE (see also Maps 5 & 8)

1 BAMFORD   Derwent (B 395)
Bass. Small late-Victorian hotel. B & B.
Meals day and evening. Overgrown
bowling green. Family room off main
entrance.
In village centre between A57 and A625
on B6013.

2 ROWSLEY   Goose & Claret
(Darley Dale 3233)
Mansfield. Large stone building once a
coaching house. B & B. Lunches, snacks
in the evenings. Garden. Sun verandah
off car park used as family room with
access to lounge.
On A6 N of Matlock.

3 WENSLEY   Crown (Darley Dale 2598)
Marstons. 18th C pub with fine views.
Roadside parking in market square. Light
snacks. Garden, patio with swings.
Games room off main entrance used as
family room. Traditional beer.
In village centre off B5057 off A6.

4 MATLOCK Dale Road   Boathouse
(M 3776)
Hardy & Hanson. Much added to stone
pub once used by quarry boats. B & B.
Lunches and evening meals daily. Patio
with swings. Family room, use of lounge
through main bar. Traditional beer.
On A6 S end of town, overlooking river.

**5 GRANGE MILL (nr Wirksworth)
Holly Bush** (Winster 300)
Free House. Old farmhouse converted.
Meals available all times. Garden.
Children's/family room off car park or
main bar. Traditional beer.
On A5012 Matlock/Buxton road.

**6 BROADHOLME (nr Belper)
Fisherman's Rest** (Belper 5518)
Marstons. Small 16th C village pub.
Roadside parking. Snacks in summer.
Garden and field. Children's room off car
park at back. Traditional ale.
Off A6 ½m N of Belper.

7 SCARCLIFFE   Horse & Groom
(Chesterfield 823152)
Home brewery. Old farmhouse. Home
snacks. Garden with swings, off which
is covered verandah used for family
room. Traditional beer. Out in the wilds.
4m from J29 M1 on B6417.

8 WEST HALLAM   Newdigate Arms
(Ilkeston 320604)
Allied. Large coaching house. Bar meals.
Garden with games. Verandah closed in
off the garden and small room inside for
families. Garden patio with swings.
Off A609 in centre of village. NW of
Ilkeston on A610.

NOTTINGHAMSHIRE (see also Map 5)

**9 NUTHALL, Nottingham Road
Three Ponds** (Nottingham 383170)
Hardy & Hanson. Typical friendly village
local. Lunches Mon-Fri. Snacks other
times. Garden with large covered
verandah for wet days for families.
In village centre ¼m from J26 M1.

**10 NEWARK-ON-TRENT Kirkgate
Old King's Arms** (N 3416)
Free House. Old 17th C compact house.
Town car park nearby. Lunches (except
Sun). Large family room to right upstairs.
Traditional beer.
Off A46, in town centre to church. One-
way street.

11 BLYTH   Angel (B 213)
Free House. One-time coaching house of
note. B & B. Restaurant, bar meals. Garden. Family room with games off entrance hall. Traditional beer.
½m off A1M on B1064 in village centre.

LINCOLNSHIRE (see also Map 6)

12 TORKSEY   Castle (T 212)
Home brewery. One-time farmhouse.
B & B. Basket meals all times. Patio. Old
barn used as family room with games,
and own soft-drinks bar (generally Fri
and Sat eve but available other times).
Traditional beer (electric pumps).
On A156 Gainsborough road. S of Gainsborough, half-way to Lincoln.

13 SAXILBY   Vine (Skegness 72228)
Home brewery. Victorian corner pub.
Meals all times. Patio in car park and use
of private room (with TV) in evenings
only. Traditional ale.
In village centre off A57. NW of Lincoln.

**14 WASHINGBOROUGH High Street
Ferry Boat** (Lincoln 790220)
Watneys. Ferrymen's house of yesteryear. Snacks available. Garden with
swings. Large meeting room used as
family room off corridor to bar with toys.

MAP 9

Just off B1190 in village centre. E of Lincoln.

15 INGOLDMELLS Hastings Corner Cherry Tree (Skegness 2756)
Hardy & Hanson. Large modern seaside pub. Lunches daily in lounge. Basket meals evenings. Seats outside. Large family room off car park with games. Off Roman bank of A52 Mablethorpe road. N of Skegness.

16 CHAPEL ST LEONARDS Vine (Skegness 72228)
Bass. A large between-wars pub on the green. Accommodation. Lunches. Patio. Large family room off main bar with own servery.
On A52 in village centre. N of Skegness.

17 HOGSTHORPE Mill Lane Victoria (Skegness 72815)
Batemans. Victorian pub, hence name. Bar snacks. Garden. Children's room in old stable during season, with games and own bar attendant. Use of pool room in winter. Traditional beer.
Just off A52 in village centre, half-way between Skegness and Mablethorpe.

18 HUTTOFT Axe Cleaver (Boston 63129)
Batemans. Small cottage-type pub. Snacks. Garden with swings and goat. Children's bar off garden. Camping site. Traditional beer.
On A52 in village centre. S of Mablethorpe.

19 MABLETHORPE Cross Inn (M 7204)
Bass. Modern cottage-type pub enlarged. Bar snacks (not Sun). Small garden with amusements. New family room with soft-drinks bar in summer, off car park.
On junction A1104/A1031. W side of Mablethorpe.

20 MABLETHORPE Lively Lady (M 2316)
Free House. A modern brick house. Snacks. Patio. Separate children's room alongside.
On road out of town to Withem.

UMBERSIDE

21 WESTWOODSIDE (nr Doncaster) Park Drain (Hoxey 752255)
Free House. Massive, known as 'Klondyke'. Snacks. Fishing, patio. Children's room with games off main hall.

Just off B1396 in the wilds. NW of Gainsborough.

22 BELTON Crown
Darley. Tiny farmhouse converted. Old-fashioned brick pub. Small play area. Small room off main bar used for families in wet weather. Traditional beer.
Off A161 2m from M180, by church.

23 RAWCLIFFE Riverside Rose & Crown (Goole 83422)
Allied. Small waterside pub. Snacks. Orchard. Family room off main bar for wet weather. Traditional ale.
Off A614 to river.

SOUTH YORKSHIRE

24 HATFIELD WOODHOUSE Green Tree (Doncaster 84035)
Darley. Old farmhouse, well converted. Restaurant evenings (except Mon). Bar meals. Garden. Family room off main entrance, new restaurant. Traditional beer.
On A614, 2½m from J5, M18.

25 HOLLOW MEADOWS (nr W Sheffield)
* Norfolk Arms (Sheffield 301781)
Allied. One-time private house, then coaching stage. Lunches Mon-Fri. Light snacks other times. Garden with numerous amusements. Family room with access from garden, and small family room with games. Traditional beer.
On main A57 overlooking reservoir.

WEST YORKSHIRE (see also Map 8)

26 WHITWOOD (nr Castleford) Rising Sun (Castleford 554766)
Allied. Castle-like tower on end of bungalow-type building. Bar snacks. Large verandah room off car park, used as family room. Traditional beer.
On A655, ½m N of J31 M62.

27 ECCUP New Inn (Harlwood 886335)
** Allied. Private house greatly enlarged. Lunches Mon-Fri. Snacks other times. Garden, playground with house and peacocks. Large new family room off car park with amusements. Traditional beer.
E off A650 in hills, N of Leeds.

NORTH YORKSHIRE (see also Map 8)

28 CARLTON Foresters (Goole 860254)

MAP 9

Free House. 18th C one-time home of the Ancient Order. Snacks. Conservatory with ancient vine used as family room. Traditional beer.
On A1041 in village centre.

29 WIGHILL White Swan
** (Tadcaster 832217)
Free House. Attractive stone building. Snacks. Patio in front with games room off and a family room lunchtime and to 8pm in evenings. Traditional beer.
Off A64, 2m from Tadcaster in village centre.

30 KEARBY (nr Kirkby Overblow)
** Clapgate (Harewood 8863181)
Allied. Large rambling private house converted. Bar meals (not Mon). Snacks other times. Garden with house and swings. Large family room off garden. Caravan site. Traditional beer.
On minor roads, 5m W of Wetherby, 2m W off A661.

31 LOWER MARISHES School House
(Kirby Misperton 247)
Free House. One-time Victorian school. B & B, snacks. Small pretty garden. Lounge used as family room.
E off A169 in small hamlet.

32 STAXTON Hare & Hounds
(Sherburn 243)
Bass. Old coaching farmhouse. B & B. Snacks. Garden with swings. Family room off main bar and car park.
On A64 at junction with B1249, W of Filey.

33 FILEY Three Tuns (Scarborough 512192)
Camerons. Modernised 3-storey town-centre pub on road to sea. Snacks. Children's bar off entrance and lounge bar.
In town centre off A1039 on road to sea.

34 LEBBERSTON Boak End Plough
(Scarborough 582224)
Camerons. Old red-brick smallholding of yesteryear. Snacks. Small children's room with numerous games off back entrance. Traditional beer.
On A165, isolated.

35 NOSTERFIELD Free Masons (Well 348)
Free House. 18th C local rough stone. B & B, snacks. Small family room off main entrance. Traditional beer.
On B6267 Thirsk/Masham road, 4m E of Masham.

36 BURNESTON (nr Bedale) Woodman
(Bedale 2997)
Camerons. Small 19th C house on old coaching route. Snacks. Family room at front entrance. Traditional beer.
Just off A1 in village centre. S of Catterick.

37 BEDALE Market Square White Bear
(B 2518)
Camerons. 17th C coaching house with market licence Tues and Thurs. B & B. Bar meals every day. Patio in yard. Family room off main entrance passage opposite bar. Traditional beer.
In town centre on A684/B6268 junction, E of Northallerton.

MAP 9
Other pubs to try

DERBYSHIRE (see also Maps 5 & 8)

ASHOVER (nr Chesterfield) Black Swan Small games room off lounge
BARLOW Peacock Play area
BASLOW (nr Bakewell) Robin Hood Garden, play area
CALVER Derwentwater Arms Play area
DARLEY DALE Holly Bush Garden, play area, views
DUFFIELD Bridge Riverside terrace
ECKINGTON (Marsh Lane) Fox & Hounds Garden, play area
GRASSMOOR Boot & Shoe Play area
ILKESTON Anchor Children's facilities, garden
PENTRICH Dog Children's facilities
WINDLEY Puss in Boots Garden with swings

NOTTINGHAM (see also Map 5)

BLIDWORTH Fox & Hounds Swings and see-saw

MAP 9

EPPERSTONE **Cross Keys** Swings
GUNTHORPE **Unicorn** Play area
LOWDHAM **World's End** Garden with amenities
NEWARK **Ram** Children's facilities
NOTTINGHAM **Trip to Jerusalem** Famous historic caves, garden
OXTON **Green Dragon** Play area
PINXTON **Boat** Riverside
PINXTON **Miner's Arms** Play area
PLEASLEY **Nag's Head** Swings and frame
RAVENSHEAD (nr Kirkby in Ashfield) **Little John** Play area
RETFORD **Elms** Children's facilities and play area
RETFORD **Hop Pole** Canalside garden
STOKE BARDOLPH **Ferry Boat** Riverside garden
WOODBOROUGH **Nag's Head** Swings and frame

LINCOLNSHIRE (see also Map 6)

ALFORD **Half Moon** Children's facilities, twice monthly folk club
BRACEBRIDGE HEATH **Blacksmith's Arms** Swings, slides and frame
HORNCASTLE **Bull** Children's facilities, monthly folk club
MABLETHORPE **Fulbeck** Children's facilities and garden
MALTBY-LE-MARSH **Crown** Children's facilities
SPILSBY **George** Children's facilities and garden
WITHERN **Red Lion** Children's facilities and garden
WRAGBY **Turner's Arms** Children's facilities and garden

HUMBERSIDE

PAULL (Hull) **Humber Tavern** Garden overlooking river
PAULL (Hull) **Royal Oak** Children's facilities and garden
SEWERBY (Bridlington) **Ship** Children's playground
SOUTH FERRIBY **Hope & Anchor** Riverside garden
SWINEFLEET (Goole) **King's Head** Riverside garden

SOUTH YORKSHIRE

CAWTHORNE **Spencer Arms** Swings
FINNINGLY (nr Doncaster) **Harvey Arms** Garden and village green
HOYLAND NETHER **Furnace** Garden and village pond
MEXBOROUGH **Ferry Boat** Canalside
SPROTBROUGH **Ivanhoe** Cricket field
SWINTON **Traveller's Rest** Children's facilities

WEST YORKSHIRE (see also Map 8)

DURKAR **Navigation** Canalside garden
FERRYBRIDGE **Golden Lion** Riverside
HAVERCROFT (nr Royston) **Eagle** Play area, Bank Holiday amusements
RODLEY **Railway** Canalside garden
UPPER HOPTON **Flower Pot** Riverside

NORTH YORKSHIRE (see also Map 8)

ACASTER MALBIS **Ship** Riverside
CATTERICK **Oak Tree** Village green
ELVINGTON **Grey Horse** Village green

MAP 9

FILEY   Foords   Children's facilities and garden
HARROGATE   St George   Children's facilities
HARROGATE   Traveller's Rest   Large play area
HAWSKER   Hare & Hounds   Lawns and play area
HELMSLEY   Crown   Children's area and room
HESLINGTON (nr York)   Dexamore Arms   Swings and rocking horse
HORNBY BRIDGE   Bingley Arms   Canalside
KNARESBOROUGH   Mother Shipton   Riverside
NETHER POPPLETON (York)   Fox   Riverside garden
NEWTON-ON-OUSE   Blacksmith's Arms   Orchard
OSWALDKIRK   Malt Shovel   Ornate gardens
RIPON   Wheatsheaf   Peacocks
ROBIN HOOD'S BAY   Victoria Hotel   Sea views
RUSWARP   Unicorn   Play area
SCARBOROUGH   Cask   Children's facilities and gardens
SCORTON   Royal   Village green
SHERBURN   Pigeon Pie   Children's facilities
SOUTH MILFORD (nr Leeds)   Selby Oak   Children's playground
STAINTONDALE   Shepherds Arms   Garden overlooking sea
STAPLETON (Darlington)   Bridge   Garden on village green
TADCASTER   Royal Oak   Children's facilities
THIRSK   Boot & Shoe   Play area and camping
THORNTON DALE   Hall   Children's facilities, large gardens with lawn
WHITBY   Market   Backs on to harbour
YEDINGHAM   Providence   Children's area

CLEVELAND (see also Map 10)

EAGLESCLIFFE (nr Yarm)   Pot & Glass   Patio, playground

DURHAM (see also Map 10)

NEASHAM (Darlington)   Newbus Arms   Children's facilities and large garden

MAP 10

CUMBRIA (see also Map 8)

1 SPRINGFIELD (nr Troutbeck)
Sportsman (Greystoke 231)
Jennings. Isolated farm cottages converted with views over valley. B & B.
Restaurant (evenings). Bar meals. Patio garden. Large family/games room off main bar and restaurant. Traditional beer.
S off A66 W of Penrith. 8m W of J40 M6.

2 THRELKELD   Horse & Farrier (T 688)
Jennings. 17th C pub used by Wordsworth. Bar snacks. Garden. Small snug off main bar used as family room. Traditional beer.
S off A66 in village centre.

3 HIGH LORTON   Horseshoe (HL 214)
Jennings. Quaint old house. Meals. Small room off bar used as family room. Traditional beer.
1½m W off A66 in village centre, in cul-de-sac.

4 ROWRAH   Stork (Ramplugh 213)
Jennings. Old coaching stage in hamlet. Draw in. B & B. Sandwiches. Children allowed in the lounge upstairs used as family room. Traditional beer.
On A5086 N end of village.

5 BRANTHWAITE   Star
(Workington 2520)
Jennings. Small 17th C pub with coaching associations. Restaurant evenings (to order). Snacks. Family room off the entrance passage. Traditional beer.
Off A595 in village.

6 EMBLETON   Wheatsheaf
(Bassenthwaithe Lake 488)
Jennings. One-time farmhouse. B & B. Basket meals. Garden. Small family room off main bar (also games room). Traditional ale.
N off A66 E of Cockermouth in village.

7 ASPATRIA Outgang Road   Letters Inn
(A 20448)
Jennings. Victorian pub. Beer garden. Small family room off main entrance. Traditional beer.
On B5301 in town centre.

8 BOLTON LOW HOUSES
Oddfellows Arms (Wigton 2049)
Village meeting house for centuries. Bar meals (evenings until 8.30pm). Garden. Comfortable family

room at back. Traditional beer.
Just off A595 in village centre.

9 ROCKCLIFFE   Metal Bridge
(R 206)
Scottish & Newcastle. One-time farm. Restaurant. Bar meals. Garden with fishpond. Coffee room off main entrance used as children's/family room. Traditional beer.
Alongside A74 just N of Carlisle overlooking River Esk.

10 TALKIN   Hare & Hounds
(Brampton 3456)
* Free House. Quiet village pub. B & B, bar meals all times. Beer garden. Family room off the main bar at the back. Traditional beer.
S off B6413 in small village 8m E of J43, M6.

DURHAM & CLEVELAND

11 WEST AUCKLAND The Green
Prince of Wales
(Bishop Auckland 832277)
Camerons. Old miners' pub, the court house. Roadside parking. B & B. Snacks. Family room off passage entrance (also games room). Traditional ale.
On A68 in centre of village.

12 WHEALEY GREEN (nr Edmondsley)
* **Charlaw** (Stanley 32085)
Free House. Red-brick with views. Restaurant, bar meals. Garden with swings. Family room off lounge bar with suntrap.
In the wilds in small hamlet off B6532.

13 WHITE-LE-HEAD (nr Stanley)
Tantobie Bird (Stanley 32416)
Free House. Old coaching house on top of hill. Bar meals every day. Room off main bar used as family room until 8pm. Traditional beer.
On B6311 just off A692. N of Stanley.

NORTHUMBERLAND

14 CORBRIDGE Middle Street   Black Bull
(C 2261)
Whitbread. 16th C squat stone building. Restaurant. Bar lunches. Family room through main bar used as coffee room.
On A68 on one-way system in town centre.

15 CORBRIDGE   Wheatsheaf (C 2020)

MAP 10

Vaux. One-time coaching house. B & B. Snacks daytime. Sun lunch. Garden. Two rooms one with TV, used as family rooms. Traditional beer.
On A68 in town centre.

16 FEATHERSTONE   Wallace Arms
(Haltwhistle 20375)
Free House. Rough granite. Accommodation. Meals. Small garden. Snug bar on right of passage used as family room. Traditional beer.
2½m off A69 on road to Featherstone Park.

17 HALTWHISTLE   Grey Bull (H 20298)
Free House. Large Victorian granite building. B & B. Bar meals. Family room in lounge with TV, off main hallway. Traditional beer.
Off A69 in town centre.

**18 FORESTBURN GATE (nr Rothbury)
Crown & Thistle** (Rothbury 20643)
Free House. Isolated farm cottage converted. Snacks. Seats outside and small room off main bar for families.
On B6342 4m S of Rothbury.

MAP 10
Other pubs to try

CUMBRIA (see also Map 8)

ALLONBY   Grapes   Children's facilities, garden, views
APPLEBY   Grapes   Children's facilities, opposite river
CARLISLE   Turf   Old racecourse and donkey
CROSBY   Lonsdale   Children's facilities
WYTHOP   Pheasant   Children's facilities, garden

CLEVELAND (see also Map 9)

BROTTON   Ship   Children's facilities
HART (nr Hartlepool)   Raby Arms   Swings and roundabouts

DURHAM (see also Map 9)

BARNARD CASTLE   Raby   Children's facilities
CORNFORTH   Square & Compass   Village green
DARLINGTON   White Horse   Play area
EGGLESTON (nr Barnard Castle)   Three Tuns   Play area
HIGHER CONISCLIFFE (nr Darlington)   Spotted Dog   Village green
PIERCEBRIDGE   Wheatsheaf   Children's facilities
SEDGEFIELD   Nag's Head   Village green
WESTGATE   Hare & Hounds   Play area and camping
WOODLAND   Royal   Garden with views

TYNE-TEES

FENCE HOUSES (nr Chester-le-Street)   Station   Children's facilities and garden
MARSDON (S Shields)   Marine Grotto   Waterside frontage
NEWCASTLE   Time Out   Children's facilities
NORTH HYLTON   Shipwright's Arms   Riverside

NORTHUMBERLAND

BERWICK   Hen & Chickens   Children's facilities
GREENHEAD   Blenkinsop Castle   Private gardens
GREENHEAD   Greenhead   Children's facilities and garden
MITFORD (nr Morpeth)   Plough   Play area, swings, birds
NEWSHAM   Black Diamond   Children's facilities
STAMFORD (nr Alnwick)   Mason's Arms   Play area
STANNINGTON   Ridley Arms   Goldfish pond